WE HAVE ALL GONE AWAY

A Bur Oak Book

We Have All Gone Away

CURTIS HARNACK

UNIVERSITY OF IOWA PRESS • IOWA CITY

University of Iowa Press, Iowa City 52242
www.uiowapress.org
First published by Doubleday & Company, Inc., 1973
First University of Iowa Press edition, 2011
Printed in the United States of America

The University of Iowa Press is a member of Green Press Initia-
tive and is committed to preserving natural resources.

Printed on acid-free paper

Library of Congress Cataloging-in-Publication Data
Harnack, Curtis, 1927–
We have all gone away / by Curtis Harnack.—1st University of
Iowa Press ed.
p. cm.
"A Bur Oak book."
ISBN-13: 978-1-58729-969-8, ISBN-10: 1-58729-969-0 (pbk.)
ISBN-13: 978-1-58729-970-4, ISBN-10: 1-58729-970-4 (e-bk.)
1. Harnack, Curtis, 1927—Childhood and youth. 2. Authors,
American—20th century—Biography. 3. Farm life—Iowa.
4. Iowa—Social life and customs. I. Title.
PS3558.A62474Z476   2011   2011002349
813'.54—dc22
[B]

For Paul E. Triem

WE HAVE ALL GONE AWAY

1. *The Return*

In a cab bound for the East Side Airlines Terminal, where I was to check in for my flight to Iowa, a long traffic light on Forty-second Street gave me a chance to look up at the skies to see what the weather was like, for now that I was about to leave the city, I'd be encountering it again. I happened to notice a sign on a structure behind Times Square: THIS BUILDING TO BE DEMOLISHED IDEAL BUSINESS SITE WILL BUILD TO SUIT. I studied the nineteenth-century stone and brick edifice for whatever architectural interest it might have—to take one last look along with my first. The gray, beaten-metal cornice eight stories up suddenly took shape. I saw a caryatid mounted on each corner, then another and another, spaced every twenty feet or so: enormous barn owls in fluted copper, their faces keen to the beak, with magnificent ruffs and blind eyes; their wide-spread wings seemed to hold up the roof.

The taxi pulled away fast, as if the driver felt he knew better than I how very late it was. The building would be gone in a week or a month, the owls destroyed, and I wondered if I'd been the last person to recognize what they were. It was a familiar city feeling. I tried to accept the imminent departure of those metal barn owls roosting over Times Square as an inevitable fact of urban life, a consequence of the passage of time. I was almost used to the ravage of the bulldozer, the iron ball, the jackhammer, and paralyzed into accepting their necessity. It was growth, economic life—it was change.

Even the Sioux City airport showed signs of this feverish urge for difference usually called progress: it had Hertz car service, a curved glass observatory with a restaurant attached, and the old Floyd Monument, an obelisk of stone on the banks of the Missouri, had a fiercely blinking light on top of it now for safety's sake. And was that ramshackly Ford into which I hastily flung my suitcase really my uncle's new car of four years ago? Had I changed so much that his slightly quizzical and guarded expression meant *could this be you?* Had he in turn not gotten considerably grayer? In a minute—or a day—it would not seem so, but I caught the turned-under moment for what it was, before we presented ourselves to each other, right side up.

We drive the forty miles through flat farmland and tiny railroad towns to reach home. "Want to see the new post office?" he says, slowing down as we arrive.

"Other one torn down?" I ask, remembering with a pang the funny clapboard building, slim metal pillars at the entrance, and the immense storefront window for those outside to see easily who was inside, and vice-versa.

"Sure—it's a medical center now."

"A *what?*" The town has only one thousand two hundred people.

"The medical center. See?"

A one-story yellow brick building, doctor in one wing, dentist in the other, with, I suppose, a waiting room in the middle which made it a "center." I turn to him: "Very nice, but where's the post office?"

"I'll show you." We're there, two blocks away, in a minute. "Government built that—didn't cost the town anything."

It appears alien in this setting: another lean, narrow-brick affair with tropical-looking louvered windows high under the cropped eaves. Fluorescent lights glare with a white, operating-room intensity, and I am told that the formica counters are blue, the floor red. Thousands of these red, white, and blue post offices across the country, all exactly alike. "We're keeping up with the times here in a few ways, you might say." He sets the Ford in motion again. "We've even got a supermarket, where the old Grand Theatre used to be. I'll let you take a look."

The cinema where I'd seen my first movie had originally been a Catholic church, a fact which in childhood always intrigued me. I wondered if the ticket taker's booth had been the confessional. Now the frame building had been razed and a cinder-block grocery stood on the spot. Apparently it had been impossible to shift from a celluloid film business to one concerned with plastic-wrapped food; or, in the old days, did these adaptations take place because nobody had the money or knowledge to do it differently—and so a church was converted into a theater? I tell my uncle that the supermarket looks as modern as anything I've seen in Westchester or Long Island.

And that parking lot, what used to be there? "Wasn't some blacksmith's shop right about here?"

He glances at me sharply: "You—how do *you* remember that? Was that thing still standing when you were a kid?"

"I used to watch the sparks fly when the blacksmith pounded a red-hot shoe into shape, on the anvil. And the wonderful *sssssst* it made when he threw it into a tub of water. I even held the horse, once. Of course I remember."

"No!" he murmurs, smiling, but he doesn't want to take the memory farther. Up ahead on the corner is a brand-new pink house, beautifully landscaped. "They put that house up in three days, shrubs and all. I saw 'em do it. All prefab."

Still, when we reached the farmhouse it was much the same, only shabbier and badly in need of paint, inside and out. He lived alone and rented out most of the land: in one fashion or another his seven children had gone, by way of learning, wars, and marriage—the American way. He would by now have torn out the old, partially modernized kitchen and put in a Youngstown stainless steel one, if he'd had the money to do it, or the inclination; but there was no woman to cook or care for him, and no reason therefore not to continue with the wooden kitchen cabinet with its slatted roll-door compartment, no excuse to put down vinyl tiles in spangled purple over the pine floor that had been laid by his father nearly a hundred years ago. Except for a new television set on a tubular brass, plastic-wheeled cart, the old furniture was still around, arranged as it had been for four decades. Here time had stopped, but it was not to be recognized or commented upon. We were not going to be sad about anything. Yes, there were cobwebs across the windows and plaster had fallen from some upstairs ceilings—part of the house had been closed off and not swept or waxed for years—but no matter. My uncle told me he had plans for tearing off the front porch in order to make a carport. Handier, it would be, getting from car to house, especially in winter. He was not a man ever to complain about the ravages of change. He went it one better: he did the changing.

That was the way he always was, even in my earliest recollections. Such disasters as the death of my father—his brother— were never mulled over or discussed because the thing was past and over and what point would there be in it? We were all taught to lean enthusiastically into tomorrow, when we would be tall enough for basketball, strong enough to run the tractor and plant corn, old enough to travel to distant cities such as Chicago and see what was new in the world. That was how we burned up the years: but in my uncle's view, how could it ever be otherwise—and who'd want it to be?

I mark the moment I first knew this when I became old enough to accompany the rest of the family on an overnight fishing trip to "the lakes," a cluster of ponds and sizable spring-fed lakes just south of the Minnesota border. The excursion was to be a surprise for me and my younger cousin; we were encouraged to hope for sudden, exquisite moments of joy. At Christmas time Santa Claus left miraculously appropriate gifts under the tree, and in spring the Easter Rabbit put chocolate eggs in our carefully contrived nests. On birthday mornings there were presents hanging from one's chair at the table, or under the breakfast plate. And on summer evenings we'd take spontaneous automobile rides which ended in an ice-cream parlor in a nearby town. Awakened in the middle of the night by a glow coming through the transom from a parent's bed light, one might easily mistake a visit to the bathroom for predawn stirrings in preparation for a journey to visit cousins who lived in eastern Iowa. We children were urged to believe in the arbitrary appearance of unspeakable pleasures—and sometimes it led us to dream of the impossible.

On my first fishing trip the whole house was illuminated at 2:30 A.M. and the shouts of the children echoed my uncle's first rousing call up the stairs: "Let's go fishing!" Never in other years had it been possible for the doors to be flung open so noisily, the talk to be out loud—for usually the fishing party had managed to sneak out without waking me or my young cousin, and we'd arise hours later keenly disappointed to discover the deception, left with a judgment, clear and awful: *too young.*

In the kitchen my mother and aunt were stuffing hampers with sandwiches, potato salad, and other provisions; there were field jugs of lemonade and two thermos bottles of coffee. Under the glow of the yard light at the foot of the sidewalk my uncle strapped the cylindrical ice chest to the rear bumper of the '34 Ford. The fishing poles, bait, and other gear were stashed in the small rectangular trunk, the canvas tent on top, folded as tightly as a foot soldier's pack. I always thought the tent had somehow come from those days of the World War my uncle so often talked about, as did his boots and leggings he still occasionally wore, and the cartridge belt he buckled on during pheasant-hunting season.

We piled into the car, stacked ourselves on laps, and felt the first thrill of direction, for what had formerly been only a road gate was now the beginning of a northerly route. We were going to Trumbull Lake, about which my uncle had heard good fishing reports, though not many people knew of the place. In these days of state-stocked lakes and overfished waters, a little craftiness was necessary. My uncle enjoyed the confidences of the best local fishermen, plus the game warden, and so we expected to bring home a couple dozen bullheads. The usual angler's hope of tying into an enormous fish was not part of our dreams, since there were only small perch, sunfish, bluegills, and bullheads in these waters. We were after meat—the bullheads on the bottom.

On the eighty-mile journey, I remember the serious faces of the older boys, their fisherman concerns of whether they had enough hooks and bobbers along, or had dug enough worms yesterday. Plunging pitchforks into the earth behind the barn, they had beat upon the long handles until the ground vibration sent the worms to the surface. Now that the August sun was rising, diminishing by each minute the prime fishing time, they squirmed in eagerness. They were not interested in playing the usual car game of seeing who could first spot a mule or a white horse—the announcement to be made by touching forefinger to lips, then to the palm of the hand, followed by a clap of the hand and a cry: "One white horse!" or "There's an old mule!"

The approach to a viaduct which lifted the pavement above a railroad track was hailed with great excitement. I had never really experienced a hill before; the highest I'd been was in the sparrow-infested cupola of the barn. The ascent was purposefully slow, my uncle turning around to witness my reaction—and that of his daughter, also a novice, at the other window—while my aunt said nervously, "Watch the road!" Since there were no cars behind, we paused at the very top and looked down on the ribbon of track which penciled itself out and disappeared at the horizon, in a line as straight as it must have been on the engineer's map.

"No train in sight—too bad," said my uncle, for the supreme pleasure would be to have a smoke-belching steam engine pass right under the car; but only my uncle had ever enjoyed that wonderful sensation. Slowly, as the car began its descent, the vista closed in again in the old way, and something I had long anticipated was over. Memory of it would be sealed in time, forever tantalizing but uncapturable. Even then my uncle and I were different in our views of the meaning of occurrences, for on the return trip he expected my excitement to be much the same as it had been before. Since we approached from the opposite direction, the scenery was different, and we did not pause on top at all but plunged right over—giving me a strange, sinking sensation in the pit of my stomach, as the fall began. It was fun, but I remembered what the first time over the viaduct had been like—better than this—but more important, quite surely different.

As we approached the lake country the air began to smell of water. I saw a sharp-beaked blue bird with dangling legs and a wing flap like a shaken rag. Red-winged blackbirds honkereed in the marshy hollows, and there were sloughs of tall, waving grass, acres of scrub brush and weeds: land that looked as if it had no useful purpose at all. I'd never seen uncultivated, abandoned stretches like this, and it was as much a sign of the freedom of our holiday as fishing itself—it was a field on holiday, gone wild with vegetation and bemused by blackbirds.

In the front seat, the oldest boy helped my uncle look for the Trumbull Lake turnoff, which was not even a real road, merely a lane. "There's the sign in the fence!" he shouted at last. Unlike the official highway markers, black lettering on white, this was a raw board wedged into the top wires of the fence, with "Trumbull Lake" written in blood-colored paint, as if done by a pirate. The name of the lake, the "Trum" part, had a faintly thunderous quality, but the "bull" merely suggested the bullheads on the bottom waiting for us.

"The water's high," said my uncle approvingly, as we topped a hill and saw the two-mile-long body of water lying there, so incredibly blue and strange—as if the sky had been torn down and was resting among the hills. The lake moved and flashed in the sunlight, alive and self-contained, superior to creatures of the earth such as me—and I was afraid of it. The rest of my family could scarcely refrain from leaping out of the moving car in their eagerness to run to the shore and wade in. They longed to be surrounded by water, submerged in it, cooled and slaked at last; water to their minds was one of the absolutely good things of life. Indeed, the minister in church prayed for rain almost every Sunday of the summer, for there seldom was quite enough to ensure good crops. And at the baptismal font we all had water poured over our week-old brows. On Saturday nights we were careful to bathe in each other's water, for it was too precious to be wasted on a single dirty child. At the well pump in the front yard we never threw away water if we couldn't gulp down a whole dipperful—it was carefully tossed on the Canterbury bells or rosebushes. Even when we "made water" in summer we ran into the grove, to avoid a wasteful toilet-flushing in the house.

Now in contrast to all that penurious thinking about water was a sprawling immense quantity of the stuff which couldn't be thought of in dipper terms, or even buckets and bathtubs; it was an element equal to the land and maybe mightier, since it could pull you under and drown you. I had learned to walk; now I must learn to swim; then fly—and then what? I looked at Trumbull Lake and knew I must stretch myself, leaving former certainties behind—with the earth that had appeared so immutable, but that had an adversary, too.

Quick! Out with the fishing poles, lines into the water! We had to have bullheads for lunch. Casting was like throwing a ball, said my uncle. Let the sinker fly out and don't clamp your thumb on the reel or there'll be a backlash. He strung a worm on his hook and in one powerful movement sent it singing in a high, looping arc, *plop,* fifty yards away. Then he rested his rod on a Y-branch and moved on. The other boys had rolled up their overalls and were standing in water as far from shore as they could manage, poles like whips in front of them—they were motionless. I held the rod with immense expectation, my finger alertly on the pulse of the line, waiting for that throb from the other end. Twice I reeled in frantically, triumphantly proclaiming a fish, until my uncle began to frown and warn me that I ought to be more sure of what I was doing. It was my own pounding bloodstream I felt in the pressure of my fingers.

Other interesting things half caught my attention. A farmer from the house a quarter-mile away came and talked with my uncle, who, I learned years later, paid a dollar for the camping and fishing privileges. Hose-necked water birds flew over with loud cries. The water sucked and slapped the shore, and a herd of Holsteins walked to the bank to look at us. They snorted in the water like horses at a tank until my uncle shooed them away. I thought of our cows at home and that the hired man was to do all the milking this morning. But home no longer existed; the tent was our house, and this our permanent way of life. I would always be here on the edge of the lake, looking across its cool surface toward the spotty brown pastures and the farmhouse in the west. The wind came up, riffling the water and turning it gray; I was hypnotized by the subtle movement. I don't know how long I stood there, barefoot in the comfortable ooze of the bottom, three feet from shore, but suddenly my uncle said: "Reel in your line, once. Let's see your bait."

It was gone. But how could it be? Had I felt no tugging, asked my uncle? "Now pay attention, after this."

So, fishing could be work, too; and long, empty hours of waiting for something to happen.

A few minutes later my uncle jerked his pole authoritatively and began reeling in; the water on the surface boiled as the black fish fought. There were shouts of triumph from us—and from the women around the picnic baskets under the shade of the only tree. Now at last the catch was underway and we'd all be "in luck." It wouldn't matter if he didn't catch another bullhead, since he'd shown us how it was to be done. One way or another he never failed us. At Thanksgiving he usually managed to win a turkey at the American Legion raffle, or at least a goose. One year he missed out, but he correctly estimated the number of kernels of corn in a Mason jar in the show window of the implement dealer and won three mallard ducks.

I'd seen bullheads up close before, their dark slimy skins like the inside of a Concord grape, but never hanging from a hook, the tiny yellow eyes a-stare, the tail as springy as a tree branch. My uncle put my hand on the bullhead's back, telling me to clamp firmly just behind the top sticker—a prong that might puncture one's hand. I easily tore the hook out of the soft jaw-skin. Then my uncle strung the bullhead through the gills and tied the clothesline stringer to a root at the edge of the water. The fish, feeling itself back in the lake, mistook the return for real freedom and slapped and dove, fighting the tether. Then its spirit died. How quickly and certainly did it abandon hope!

By noon we had four fish, obviously not enough for a fry; we'd accumulate our catch for a big meal in the evening. As we ate out of the picnic baskets, the older boys teased me for having caught nothing, but I was too sleepy to argue and soon crawled into the back seat of the car for a nap. I awoke an hour later to the hazy yellow look of an August afternoon, and a desperate feeling that in sleeping I'd missed something. The other children had changed to bathing suits and were frolicking in the water, supervised by my uncle, who alone knew how to swim (that skill, too, had come from those fabulous Army days); he was snuffling the water, his enormous white shoulders rhythmically heaving. With a gulping splash, under he went, then leapt upright, the water flashing off him. His face was sunburned a deep red; his arms and chest were white as the underside of a bullhead; to the elbows he was as red as his neck, and his trunks were as black as his hair. The boys began jumping upon him, knocking him over. How I envied their gamboling and felt cheated that I'd been allowed merely to sleep, which could be done as well at home. I couldn't find bathing trunks anywhere —nobody had packed a pair for me. I was deemed too young for the water, too drownable, but I wouldn't hear of it. I tore off my overalls and went out into the lake in my underwear. The men of the family cheered as I came.

Soon the churned water became muddy with our antics and the women were calling that we'd been in long enough. We tried to get up to the land, but we seemed to have lost our capacity for air and solid earth. Underwater we felt as lissome as seaweed, but on the surface we could scarcely drag our limbs to shore. Our muscles had been sucked of strength; our strangely puckered, withered hands looked as they did if one stayed in the bathtub too long.

We tried to rest on blankets spread on the grass (a swarm of flies from the herd of cows had found us, alas), and then we resumed our attack on the bullheads from a new point, farther down the shore, where none of them might have heard our splashing and shouting. Almost immediately I felt the long-anticipated tug—that wild, alive thing connected to me, via this line. "I've got one! I've got one!" I shouted, reeling in as fast as I could. My oldest brother came over to stand by in case I dropped the pole in excitement. "A big one, too—the biggest!"

By six o'clock we had a dozen (three came from me), and my uncle said it was time to quit. While the boys set up the tent, which was high enough in the center for adults to stand upright and had an annex attached to one side, I watched my uncle clean the fish with his prized Swiss knife. He made an incision, cut around the head, grabbed the loose skin with a pliers, and stripped it to the tail; three carefully selected bites and the job was done. When the whole catch had been dressed, he washed them in water from the jug we'd brought along, since lake water wasn't up to our stringent standards of cleanliness. After the Sterno-can stove was lit, the fish were rolled in cornmeal and laid in the spitting butter of the frying pan. The white, sweet flesh was rather meally, delicately fish-flavored. We were told—and knew—that we were privileged to be eating a truly rare delicacy; we savored each morsel and sucked the spines.

Later, while our marshmallows on sticks fattened over the fire, my mother and aunt called our attention to the sunset and scarlet water. They tried to express the beauty of it, how the colors were changing on the surface of the lake and in the clouds stretched across the deepening sky. We looked because they said we must, but saw only a blaze of the usual sunset colors and thought nothing further about it, since we had not yet come to ask *what is a day?*

At dusk my uncle lit the smelly, wheezing kerosene lantern, so that we could all see our way as we prepared for bed. I was asleep, rolled in a quilt, before the stars came out, it being the right of the young to fall asleep hearing adult murmuring voices —and to waken to these same elders, already up and preparing the way. When I awoke the dark, oily weatherproofed underside of the tent had thousands of little holes which were brilliant with the sun, and for a few minutes I lay and stared at the twinkling stars. Then my older brother, who was my closest watcher, announced to the family that I was awake, and my uncle said I'd better get a line into the water—not gruffly, though he meant what he said: this was a fishing trip, not a sleeping one. Today our task was to fill the ice chest with bullheads to take home; we'd eat them for supper tonight at the big round kitchen table.

I scrambled out of the tent and was puzzled to see the two oldest boys standing like herons far out in the lake. "What are they standing on?" I asked.

"They found a peninsula," said my mother, who never forgot to use the words she knew from her college education. "It's just under the surface and extends way out."

They had beat the lake, using their knowledge of the land—how clever! And now, my uncle told me, they were casting into the trough of the lake bottom, right along the bed of what used to be a creek, before the whole valley filled up with water. At the time I didn't think to ask how he knew what had been here before the lake itself. "Have they caught anything?"

"Four eight-inch bullheads," he said.

Although the temperature was only sixty-nine degrees by the camp thermometer, there was a faint breeze from the southwest blowing off the lake—Oklahoma winds, my uncle called them —and the day would be hot, dry, and dusty. The wind brought a moist, lake smell; fishy and redolent of the boggy edges, which mixed pleasantly with the aroma of boiled coffee and the brisk, inoffensive smell of cattle and dung. What a place to be! I saw my uncle's Army pocket compass and asked where the single hand pointed; where was north; where was home; and just where were we in relation to the rest of the world?

The fishing was good—I caught five—and we had thirty-seven by two o'clock, when my uncle figured it was time to leave. The older boys, a hundred yards out in the lake, pretended not to hear the summons to reel in and pack up. Again and again my uncle called, and they only moaned despondently in reply. He took the tent down himself and rolled it back into its tight, soldierly pack. Slam, slam, went the trunk lid and car doors. The blankets, jugs, and all of our fishing supplies were loaded. The boys—and the great black necklace of wriggling bullheads, which had been tied to the tree root—were the last to come out of the water. Into the insulated cylinder went the fish; into the back seat of the car, the boys.

We drove slowly down the pasture lane. "Well, gang, that's the fishing for this year," said my uncle, looking over his shoulder at the lake as we reached the top of the hill. I shall never forget the resignation and keen sorrow in his eyes, the tone of his voice. His face was our face and his sadness ours.

When we got home we were flung ruthlessly into the chores of the farm. All the chicken feeders were empty, and there was no water in any of the tanks. The pump had gone off and the hired man, a recent immigrant from Holland, had not known what was the matter or how to fix it; all the livestock was in torment. The house was echoingly empty, and the dog raced madly about the yard. We descended upon our establishment and made it quickly ours once again—and ate those bullheads at the supper table as if they'd come from a far-off world too remote to be believed. My uncle, who always closed his eyes when he ate, stripped the fishbones clean and made no mention of the day. We were all strangely let down.

"There'll be other trips," my aunt and mother told us, as we whimpered crankily going to bed. "It'll be next year before you know it."

But we weren't deceived. We knew the truth about what was over and what might or might not ever come again. In succeeding years we tried other lakes, for my uncle always liked to follow up the latest fishing reports—and our good luck at Trumbull probably meant that subsequently the lake had been fished out quickly. My uncle said he'd heard nothing about Trumbull, and so we tried Silver Lake instead. It had been beautified by rock retainer walls and a state park, just completed by the WPA. The lake bottom was sandy and the park very pretty, but there were five other families camping nearby and the fishing was terrible. Lake Okoboji was famous for its walleyed pike, but you had to hire a boat, and since that was dangerous (some of us still couldn't swim) as well as expensive, we didn't go to Okoboji. Spirit Lake was farther north, bigger, but largely taken up with

shore properties and my uncle didn't know where one could fish
there. For a long time we all discussed Lost Island Lake, and its
strange name had an irresistible appeal. How could an island be
lost? Where had it gone? "Under," came the reply. "It sank out
of sight." But that year someone from our town drowned in
Lost Island Lake, and the "Lost" took on a somber meaning.
The women protested going to such a place in the wake of
tragedy, and so we took a short trip instead to an artificial lake
only forty miles away, created by a dam, and well stocked. There
were stone fireplaces and rustic picnic tables along the narrow
body of water, and spindly trees had been planted, some of them
already withered. We got a few four-inch bullheads, but it
wasn't much fun.

The following year we went for catfish in the Little Sioux
River. We didn't catch any, but the river was so close to home
that we hoped to try our luck there often, since we wouldn't
have to stay overnight. We couldn't be away from the farm that
long now because the hired man had married and left us. One of
the boys would have to remain at home to do the work. It seemed
harder and harder to squeeze in a fishing trip between the end
of threshing season and the beginning of silage-cutting.

The memory of Trumbull didn't die, however; I kept bringing
it up. Finally, the summer I was twelve, my uncle agreed to
drive to "the lakes," though he swore he'd not heard anybody
mention Trumbull in years and didn't know if he could find it.
The newest road maps didn't show it at all. "Oh, it wasn't very
big, I guess," he said. "Just a cow pond, really. Maybe we called
it Trumbull because that was the name of those people who
owned the farm nearby."

Fewer of us were to make the trip: one was dead of peritoni-
tis—my uncle's youngest son—the two oldest boys were left
home to take care of the livestock and my mother remained to
cook for them. Since the rest of us children had grown bigger,
we couldn't have all fitted into the old car anyhow; but the car
at least was the same, only shabbier. Now it was *my* duty to look
for the blood-red sign in the fence.

I couldn't find it. We backed up in roadways and traversed the same stretch of thoroughfare three times, until my uncle decided he recognized the lane, though it wasn't marked by a sign. There was a crude gate of barbed wire and laths across the entrance; I unhooked it and pushed it aside. We moved forward a couple of hundred yards to the top of a hill and saw before us only a lake of waving bluegrass where Trumbull had been.

"Could this be—" said my aunt.

"Yes, there's the farm," I answered.

"The people are gone, though," my uncle said. The house was clearly abandoned, the windows broken, and a tree was growing through the porch roof.

"I guess the lake's drained out," said my little cousin.

As we turned around and drove away, I thought my uncle must be thinking: This is what comes of trying to find your way back into the past—for he looked at me, who had been most persistent about coming again to Trumbull Lake. But instead, as soon as we were out on the road, he spoke: "I don't think that *was* Trumbull. Wasn't there a barn, too, besides a house—and a shed? I think Trumbull must be farther to the west. We must've come in the wrong way."

"We'll waste half the day lookin' for it," said my aunt. "There's Silver Lake—right over there. At least we know where we're at, and can grill our wienies on the fireplace."

And that is what we did, though my uncle continued to ruminate aloud over the whereabouts of Trumbull. But I knew that the peninsula had risen out of the water, a *found* island, and the land had taken over: and that I'd just now seen the lost lake of my childhood. But my uncle would not admit this. It wasn't that the past didn't exist—or hadn't happened—but rather that its judgments could always be postponed, as well as whatever certainty it might contain.

That is why today, as we make the rounds of the old countryside together, we lean in different directions. I am seeking the final meanings to the mystery of past happenings here. He is eager to show how the years have erased themselves as they transpired and how man has co-operated in this obliteration. He persuades me to visit a nearby town where the new wide main

street has been shorn of trees in order to make room for a couple of hundred automobiles to park at one time on Saturday
afternoons. I gaze down the wide swath of concrete at the
strangely denuded two-story brick storefronts, electricity and
telephone lines crosshatched overhead, and see only the van-
ished elms and oaks. And by this time in New York, surely the
owls have left Times Square.

2. *The Barns*

Grandfather built barns during the 1870's in the valley of the Turkey River north of Dubuque. His barns were not squat and heavy-breasted, where the roof line heaves in order to accommodate heaps of grain inside and windows break out in smiles. They rose like stranded ocean vessels out of a sea of prairie grass: solid stone and concrete foundations, neat board-and-batten sides, a canted roof pitched to slough off the heavy snows of Middle-Western winters.

But what's that little house on top? A *cupola*. The strange Latin word was hard for Anglo-Saxon tongues; difficult to imagine Grandfather responsible for this elegantly detailed dream-building—like the image the barn had of itself in grander terms. The cupola of our Lower Barn had scalloped white eaves, tilted side slats like unfurled fans (painted red), and a shell-patterned toy tin roof with a pommel-like steeple— plus a lightning rod. What's the cupola *for?* I'd ask Uncle Jack, and with a smile and shrug he'd say, "To finish off the barn— just for looks. Pa loved cupolas." It was the only frivolous thing I ever knew about Grandfather.

His sacred carpentry tools, which neatly fitted into compartments of a well-designed handmade box, remained in his close possession until his death in 1931 and now are exhibited in the local county museum. No wonder. They're lifeless implements. These planes, awls, saws, files, drill bits need further explanation. How did they work for a man? None of us can pick them up and proceed. Our flesh feels no connection with this lusterless iron and dry cellular tissue. Something is missing. We're not what our fathers were.

He'd been born in Mecklenburg, Germany, immigrated at age three with his parents to New Orleans, St. Louis, then Iowa, where his father bought a farm. He learned carpentry when a young man in order to accumulate a stake to go west with the railroad, which had received land (two miles on either side) from the government as incentive to lay tracks to Sioux City, linking that outpost on the Missouri River to Chicago six hundred miles east. Paying eight dollars an acre in gold, he claimed one hundred and sixty acres and immediately began erecting barns—the house could come later. He reserved nine acres for outbuildings, yards, orchards, groves—nine extravagant acres that would never yield crops, never "pay." All his work with cut lumber made him hungry for trees, of which there were none, and from eastern Iowa's wooded coulees he transplanted seedlings of walnut, oak, cedar, birch, maple, pine, as well as fruit trees and shrubs which have flowered each spring for the last hundred years. This barn builder had an affinity for the immortal aspects of wood, knew that Jesus, dying for the sins of the world, ensuring life-everlasting for those who believed, had done it on a cross of wood.

After the homestead was settled, Grandfather constructed a modest frame Lutheran church, where the women sat on the right, the men on the left, and listened to sermons in German. Having no hymnbooks, the clergyman sang off a phrase, the congregation repeating it—including, one Sunday: "Must have a speck on my glasses—can't see too well. Don't sing *that! Gott in himmel,* where were we, you stupid people!"

Grandfather's heart was pure and terrible. He was the stern German father of legend who hushed the children and made them work, who loved them so strongly he beat them when they were the slightest bit wicked, and who never touched a drop of liquor but kept rye whiskey in the kitchen cabinet, liniment for his achy legs, scoffing at the lushes of the neighborhood who were outraged, who'd probably, Grandfather felt, gladly lick his legs if given half a chance. Laziness, softness, and mischievousness were to be purged from children, and the sooner they learned the hard lessons of life the better. Every year in fall after corn picking his six children (a seventh died at birth) filled mattress ticks with fresh cornhusks. But little Jack complained, said why empty out the old only to put in more cornhusks, to which Grandfather replied, "You'll find out." By January the old shucks in Jack's ticking were so shredded he had nothing but lumps left, he was miserable. And Grandpa smiled.

From 1895 to 1925, those leaping years for American agriculture, his land value increased to six hundred dollars an acre and he made money on crops and herds. Only once, in the Depression of 1907, were times so tough that the family ate hand-ground cornmeal mush laced with fresh milk. Uncle Jack and my aunts, who told of the hardship, couldn't bear to have the porridge served, though we seven grandchildren insisted on tasting *at least once* this galling substance—found it delicious. Grandpa owed nobody money, never bought what he couldn't pay cash for, and so, in the midst of the 1930's Depression, there was nothing for us to fear, not even fear itself; we could eat off the land, burn wood from our huge grove, make-do with hand-me-down clothes from the attic, for nothing had ever been thrown away (on a farm there's no place to throw it), not even Grandmother's high-button shoes.

I was four when Grandfather died, and I remember him only as he looked in the dull-penny coffin, earth-still behind the lace scrim which fell from the open lid: the first dead person I'd seen, since my father, who'd succumbed three years earlier, I'd not yet heard of or even missed. No doubt I was allowed to view the corpse because the funeral proceedings were so genial. Heavy scent of funeral flowers, self-congratulatory heartiness. Grandfather, this grand octogenarian, sculpturally smooth in his repose, was actually in heaven; about such a good man there

couldn't be the slightest doubt. Hoards of relatives filled Grandfather's retirement house, which he'd designed and built by
hand with the aid of his two sons (my father and Uncle Jack),
who married two sisters and had taken over the homestead.
After such a successful life, what was there to be sad about?
Grandfather moved out and away from us on an island of
honor, the way Elijah was assumpted into the skies. Everything
he'd created here on earth was going to live on.

Behind him hovered a dimmer ancestor, Grandpa's father,
who journeyed west in *his* old age to see what his Americanized
son had achieved, to be nourished by the parade of human
progress nearing its apex with the coming of the twentieth century. But something mysterious happened to him. He was said to
have been "lost" on his return to eastern Iowa, in a snowstorm,
a cyclone, a derailing, or some prairie mishap of casually disas-
trous dimensions. His body was never found, though his tomb-
stone, which had already been purchased, was placed on our
family cemetery plot, three square-cut white marble blocks in
diminishing sizes, discolored to a blackish green under the
pines. The day before Memorial Day when I'd be mowing
around it, clipping the grass close, I always sensed nothing
there but stone. Years later as our plot filled up, we took the
meaningless marker away and Uncle Jack's daughter carved a
white lady out of it, for she was an art student. We'd come far
from pioneer barn builders and sod breakers.

Grandfather himself started our family in this aesthetic direction. When he attached wings to the farmhouse in 1900, he
paneled the doors with burled pine (flowing, unearthly faces in
the wood), laid a bird's-eye maple floor in the dining room, put
stained-glass windows in the upper slots of the bay windows,
hung globed chandeliers from the twelve foot, stamped-tin ceilings. He installed a full bathroom, a luxury surpassing most
small-town houses at the turn of the century, with a tub long
enough for the six foot men of our family to stretch out in. His
four nimble-fingered daughters pieced together quilts, embroidered tablecloths, bed linen; they could sew elaborate dresses just
by looking at magazine illustrations, create hats; they painted

watercolors and oils, enriching their old man's life with peaceful scenes of green woodlands, running brooks and waterfalls, which he'd once known; and lofty mountains he'd never see. The pictures on the walls, the linen guests used, the delicacy of the cooking, the health of the flower gardens surrounding the house were signs of a woman's worth. Years later when Uncle Jack visited me in New York for the first time, he glanced at the original watercolors and oils in my apartment and smiled, asking about my wife: "Oh, she paints too?"

Grandfather's daughters placed a kiln in the basement next to the furnace and fired hand-painted china. They persuaded their father to import quantities of pure white Haviland, Limoges, and Bavarian; while the *Lusitania* was sinking and the Huns were raping Belgium, barrels of Europe's finest bone porcelain made their way to our Iowa farm. They painted Art Deco designs, Japanese lanterns and fans, bluebirds on the wing, floral sprays, bunches of cherries on a punchbowl set, clusters of grapes on juice goblets, and blue herons and snowy egrets on vases two feet high. Each daughter decorated and fired a complete twelve-place setting of Haviland, intended for her trousseau, along with the hand-worked underwear, nightgowns, monogrammed bed linens—whole cedar chests of promise. They went off to college and could quote yards of Whittier, Bryant, Longfellow, and Lowell; traveled to California, shopped in Chicago—until they became such well-turned-out ladies no man in the neighborhood was good enough for them.

Grandfather was to blame: to have such a cultivated family was a measure of just how far he'd come—due to perseverance, hard work, and thrift. In the Upper Barn the sod breaker lay under a mantle of dust, and we children would often stare at it: an oversized plow with a deeply curved, shovel-like snout. "Yes, that's what the pioneers used," our elders said, "walking in the furrow behind it. They had oxen then, not horses, because oxen were stronger. That prairie grass was so tough nothing else could break it up. And when Grandpa built this barn you could see it for miles, the only building in sight. Neighbors came to help put it up . . . Grandpa told them what to do and later helped on *their* barns. 'Course, with no grove, the barn stood out—gold-colored new boards. How strange and high it looked!"

When the barns were finished, house construction got underway, my grandparents meanwhile living in a shack six feet wide and ten feet long called by us "the little granary," for sacks of chicken feed were sometimes kept there. Mostly it was an abandoned junk shed where hens laid eggs in impossible places, under the hand corn sheller or in a dismembered chick brooder. Such a tiny cabin, with only two windows, was a strange shelter for the beginnings of our dynasty. My ancient grandmother, who peeped at us through thick octagonal glasses, from an immense distance, spoke in a squeaky nineteenth-century voice of no resonance, and when she passed ninety, hunched over more and more into a little buttonhook—yet she'd once been tall and strong enough to labor like a man in the fields, working oxen on the family farm near the Mississippi. She recalled how her brother loped across the sod one day, frantic with the news President Lincoln had been shot. She flung down her hoe and hurried to the house, though the news was five days old, the caravan to Springfield beginning. The last time she reminisced about it, sitting on an upended orange crate near the back stoop of her house, a bottle of Pepsi-Cola in her hand, Roosevelt had just died.

And yet, with these upheavals and passings of generations, Grandfather's solid barns remained, always bearing some intimate relation to the earth. In the coulees along the Mississippi and Turkey it had been easy to nestle the barn so that a ramp on one level led into the haymow, while the animals below had their own airy prospect, unaware that in the haymow's view they were in the basement. On the flat, western Iowa prairie, however, he had to build a mound of earth to gain access to the second level, then fling a bridge across, which, underneath, would provide cover for farm machinery. The ramp made a wonderful toboggan slope—we were the only people in the township who had a hill.

Barns were the center of animal life: sows gave birth to their litters and nursed them in straw-filled pens; baby calves, though possibly born in the pasture, were imprisoned in barn compartments so that the cows released their milk to *us*. In dark corners one could unbutton trousers and no cow, pig, or swallow who saw what you were doing thought anything wrong about it. A neighbor-girl told me her parents "did it" in the barn when they went milking. There was a dirty story about Mae West, who supposedly got drunk and fell down a chute, landing under a milk cow; she looked up at the teats and said, "One at a time boys, one at a time." At barn dances couples were always slipping off "into the hay," good in the hay. And an aroused woman, arms around the waist of a bachelor, put her hand on his crotch and said, "Let's see how the barn's built."

This attraction of the barn, with its excremental smells and fecund odors, led the neighbors to hold barn dances one summer, to make a little money and have fun. They built a stairs up to the haymow door, which fell open like the rear panel of a suit of underwear. The hay itself had scratch-polished the floor so that it shone like fresh varnish. Saturday nights all summer the music came singing out of that barn until 2 and 3 A.M., with drunken brawls, fights in pigpens, couples lying in the feed bunks or away in a manger. We were prohibited from visiting this trashy scene but got a pretty good look from the ring of darkness just beyond the flood-lit yard, where all the cars were parked. In a nearby calf shed, neighbor-boy DeWayne sold Dr. Pepper, 7-Up, and other mixes for spiking drinks, keeping the beverages cool in the watering tank, beer bottles immersed in their cases like drowned toy soldiers. All this merriment was far from city ordinances and law-enforcement checkups, no questions asked about where the booze was coming from, though the state was officially dry. Soon the oldest neighbor-girl produced a healthy baby boy but no husband. When a second child arrived and became part of the family, the priest told her to stop it and find a husband at once. But the responsible fathers were clearly unavailable, and those two little bastards ran around the farm for years, cute as could be, shamefaced but pleasurable company for their grandparents, who wished no doubt it could have come about more decently but who were always on the side of life producers, of nature; and knew that everything worth while came out of a farmer's barn.

For us, even the circus. Grandfather and four of the Ringling brothers had played together as boys, put on barn stunt shows, acrobatics, in the barn lofts of the Turkey River valley. When scary-faced clowns appeared in local newspaper ads, and lions, tigers, and elephants leapt at us from billboards, we knew "the world's greatest circus," the Ringling Brothers, Barnum and Bailey, was coming for the first time to Sioux City. Uncle Jack, who'd never seen the show himself, decided we shouldn't miss this "chance of a lifetime," though grandstand seats cost a dollar for each kid. We ministered to the puzzled livestock early one evening and drove the long thirty-six miles to Sioux City. On the chicken roost planks of the grandstand, near the undulating tent top, I tried to watch everything in all three rings, pleasurably exhausted by the torment. And how amazed these city people around us would be if they knew of our special family connection to the dazzling tumult below. Had Grandfather not been so fond of hammer and saw—so practical—he might have teamed up with the Ringling boys, and by now we'd all be in the circus. Thrift, modesty, sober ambitions were not always the best virtues—extravagant longings were sometimes realized too. Days afterward, playing among the catwalk beams of the Upper Barn, we'd grab an inch-thick hay-carrier rope and swing over the bluish green mounds of safety and finally, in a daring swan dive, plummet grandly into the "net"—sending up clouds of dust, frightening the pigeons until they beat upon the window-panes to get out.

Unlike the Upper Barn, where the milking took place (the milkshed cooling tanks close to the house, the cans washed and cream separated in a room off the kitchen), the Lower Barn had nothing to do with the clean-floored, woman-proper atmosphere of home. It was the farthest building from the house, beyond a woman's yodel to come to the telephone. Barns were masculine, sensibly clean-lined, massive, smelling of grains, sweat, animals, and excrement, a composite odor no female endeavor could cope with and most sensible farmers' wives didn't try. The barn couldn't be clean enough for human habitation; no toilet training, no rules of deportment held. Even the hungry flies specked the light bulbs so thickly they had an amber glow, as if shining through tobacco juice. For all these reasons a child felt free there.

Grandfather had cunningly figured out ways to employ husbandry tactics against the livestock: pigs could be easily shunted away from their litters, boars kept from impregnating shoats, bulls from mounting the heifers, calves from sucking the milch cows. None of these animals could have what they wanted; the farmer intervened for his own purposes. Steers fattened for market, having licked clean the feed bunks until they were satiny-white, like bark-stripped cottonwoods, were driven up a surprising chute—which led into the cattle truck bound for market. The homemade chute with its lattice flooring (so that hoofs wouldn't slip on dung) looked much like one of the passageways of the barn, and the deception was never discovered by the animals until too late.

In the big alleyway below the open haymow, Grandfather had placed a wagon scale. Before farmers' co-operatives, a farmer dared not trust grain brokers in town; he had to know beforehand just how much his shipment weighed. We children played with the weights on the notched bar and jumped up and down on the floating wooden floor-scale, but nothing happened to jiggle the bar. We were of no account compared to wagon-loads of corn or oats. We couldn't make ourselves felt, next to the solid achievements of the soil.

With hay piled to the ceiling, provender for the long winter of cattle-feeding, a sheer cliff was created on the alleyway side, the hay held in place by crossbeams. Sparrows would nest there on cold nights, eyes brilliant as we shone flashlights on them, jacking sparrows, reaching in with a gloved hand to grab them and knock them senseless against the barn door, while the cats snarled and fought like jungle ancestors as they pounced; or we'd wring the birds' necks, thinking we were doing the farm good: one less sparrow eating our grain, dirtying our sills. We were hunters, savage in our male pursuits, far from the female restraints of pity and tenderness which might have weakened our quest for prey. Here we practiced shooting the BB gun, pumping up pressure to make the puny pellet strong as the rifle bullet, sparrows again the target, or sometimes even the pigeons if they were overpopulous. We were masters of the barn world; we were men.

Since the Lower Barn was nearly at sea on the plain, one could dream grandly from a high spot on the ledges near the open windows under the ridgepole at either end, but best of all was the sun-filled cupola, where we peered through slats at the rolling countryside beyond the thick grove. In this crow's-nest of a schooner, how many voyages I took! Always the higher one climbed in a tree or a barn, the greater the triumph, for only a giant could surmount the flat Middle West. We were promised we'd eventually grow tall, and each of us boys did pass six feet, but we were in a terrible hurry to achieve the tower and thus made one out of anything at hand.

Down in the pigpen compartments where the foundation was thick to keep out zero temperatures and hundred-degree heat, the straw-filled corrals each had their pig families in farrowing season, one or two sows to a pen, and I'd watch the babies slip out like sausages as the sow groaned, blue eyes rolled up in agony. How quickly the tiniest, silky-black, shivering piglet would totter to the edge of the nest and do his business, then scurry, oinking, back to the mother's nipple-studded underside. "Pigs are the cleanest animals there are," Uncle Jack would say, as if they were his own children, "and the smartest." In later years I fed hogs and came to know them personally, noting the distinctions of temperament between them. They quickly caught on to my routine chore habits and tried to outsmart me by clambering into a bushel basket of corn I'd set down carelessly. Given the chance, any pig would have become a pet and followed me around like a dog at my heels, affectionate and attentive, begging to be let in on the more interestingly diverse world of human beings. In winter I'd cook up a caldron of warm mash composed of ground feed and nutritive supplements, ladle the liquid out into the troughs, like serving soup in a Mission House. Uncle Jack believed that pigs who ate "one hot meal a day" never caught cholera. And ours didn't.

Tender as we felt toward swine, in summer a time arrived when the young boars had to be "fixed." Cutting pigs was an ugly task which embarrassed Uncle Jack; certainly the women of the house shouldn't know about it (though they did). One day two of us boys were needed in the man's world, in the barn. We'd grab a penned boar and throw him upside down on a trough on stilts, table high. He'd yell murder and let the whole farm in on the secret outrage; the barnyard roosters became alarmed and screamed, the dog barked. One boy firmly held the churning front legs, the other pulled down the kicking shanks while a strap was tightened across the animal's chest. Uncle Jack was surgeon; first a quick paintbrush dab of disinfectant on the two seminal mounds, then the incision, the testicles ripped out and strings cut and thrown to the nearby pigs, who ate these "Rocky Mountain oysters" before or after their own testicles had been removed. Then another wash of antiseptic over the wound, a further outcry from the pig, and he'd be let go, bleeding slightly at the rear but never profusely. A couple of hours later he'd be eating corn as if nothing had happened. We always did the job on wet days because there was less danger of infection, and so the air would be heavy and the odors strong— the smell as rank in the barn after we were through as if a thousand tomcats had sprayed the walls.

In air photos the Upper Barn looked like a Maltese cross, the old barn having been bisected by a new one—Grandfather's tour de force in barn-building. Six-by-six oak beams throughout created skeletal rooms which were filled with hay; the hand-whittled pegs protruding from joints made perfect rungs for barefoot grandchildren. Two chutes were on either side of the central alleyway; here hay was pitched down to the active milch cows on one side, to the dry milch cows on the other. A horse-barn chute served the stalls where Sam and Babe lived largely in retirement, hitched up only a couple times a year, in haying and threshing seasons. The barn worked on a falling principle: the lightest, best hay lay fluffily on top under bright windows on each end of the barn. Close under the roof (there was no cupola) the dust motes sparkled individually in the sun, the world was serene and ample. But underneath, the hay was older, drier, and as you descended through the chute to the ground level, you met the workings of animal intestines—shit developed, getting deeper and deeper. At last somebody had to shovel the stuff into the manure spreader, haul it to the fields, set the egg-beater rear spindle into action. Smelly gobs would fly all over the stubble fields, good for next year's corn. The whole cycle hinged upon what happened in the barn.

I searched the dim corners of the Upper Barn trying to outfox the hens, who kept eluding me with their random nests, to keep me from stealing eggs; they wanted to brood on their nests, hatch chicks, and whenever an exultant, telltale cackle arose from an odd corner of the barn, I'd try to find out where she'd laid the egg, for if a nest went undetected for five or six days— forget it, let the hen have it; or sometimes, to keep the hen producing and trying for more secret chicks, I'd heave the old eggs into the barnyard, substitute a glass egg (so she'd come back and try again). If I happened upon a light, rotten egg, well, it was as good as a bomb and one disposed of it carefully so it didn't detonate before schedule. Only absolutely fresh eggs were bartered with the grocer in town. The twelve-dozen-egg crate would be hauled to market and return filled with cans, boxes, and sacks of food; no money shown at all.

Scrambling after hens' nests, I discovered Grandfather's forgotten black walnut boards, the same kind of wood he'd used in making a desk that shut up like a chest, drawer pulls of carved acorns and oak leaves. No doubt he'd intended more cabinetmaking—table, chairs, bedstead—out of this smoky-colored old lumber from the Turkey River region. And in unused bins I found strange, antiquated machinery: a hand corn sheller, a potato digger, a cherry pitter, an apple plucker. But of all the ancient farm implements, I was most intrigued by the high, hooded buggy, black as a hearse, side flaps all the way down, covered with a fine dust that seemed the silt of the ages. Spirits

of the earlier generations dwelt there; arrested wheels con-
jured up spinning movement, and the dropped tongue suggested a time when it had been lifted to fit harnesses. The
black leather curtains with their crinkled isinglass windows, too
opaque to see through (except a slight shadow of yourself),
cloaked the presence of dead Grandfather, whose buggy this
was. If in a bold moment, urged on by a playmate, you leapt
upon the oval metal step and shoved the curtains aside, you
saw the rigidly tufted seat and the elegantly shaped rear window,
a flattened circle like the moon on the horizon—and so small!
(As if you inside wished to be hidden from the world as you
drove along, able to see only what lay in front.) What sort of
mentality enjoyed a carriage like this, and why the awful black?
Our new dark green '34 Ford, which Mother had purchased
with part of her insurance money (and learned to drive, much
to our admiration), had yellow spoke wheels and a yellow stripe
just under the wide windows, and plenty of shiny chrome trim.

Uncle Jack, born in 1896, sensed nothing fearsome in the old
buggy and so wanted to share his familiarity with this antique
that one day, after a three-inch downpour in a spring already
wet from melting snow, he hitched Sam and Babe to the buggy
and drove through the mud to pick us up at the country
school. The first child to spot the high black carriage moving
grandly into the schoolyard let out a shriek, and our teacher,
Miss Crakow, had to let up on the hard severity of preparing
us for our futures. School was over, though it was ten minutes
to four—ten minutes before she'd have given the desk bell a
shake, after consulting the watch (carefully tucked in the folds
of her dress, so that no pupil would become a clock-watcher).
We rushed to the platform in front, which was just the right
height for stepping onto the oval mesh tread of the carriage.
The film of dust had been swept away and washed by the
last of the shower; now in brilliant sunshine and in active use,
the buggy no longer seemed tomblike. On the open front seat
two of us could sit beside Uncle Jack; the rest (no, no, the
neighbor kids couldn't come—only room for us) scrambled

onto the rigid button tufts of the rear compartment and peered out the back window.

Giddyap! We were off, the aged sway-backed horses lifting their heads boisterously, like colts on the loose, playful as Uncle Jack, reveling in foolish nostalgia. The harness lay flat on their uncurried flanks, and a jeweled blue glass ornament twinkled just below each outside ear, where the straps met and passed through an ivory loop. Even the pemmican reins were soft again and Jack held them in his hands like the stems of a bouquet. This bright after-storm air had flushed time into a surprising, newborn yesterday. How the neighbor-children envied us as we drew away from the schoolhouse, the big hoop wheels spinning mud at them, a flick of triumph for us.

"Roads too bad for a car . . . couldn't get through, no, not even with the old Model T . . . chance for a buggy ride, once . . . see what it was like. . . ." But he wouldn't have had to explain anything because we accepted this bountiful surprise. Riding along in our queer barouche, everything familiar seemed freshly different. There was a softness and silence in our journey as the wheels slipped in the mud to the rhythmic splotching of the horses' hooves. We had less than a mile to our farm and, when the ride was over, disembarked at the lawn sidewalk and hurried into the house to tell the women all about it. Next day the buggy was back in the barn where it had always been kept, gathering again its mantle of dead associations, of which ours now joined our grandfather's.

When cultivating corn in the fields, I could tell time without a clock by gauging the length of shadow under the eaves of the barns. "Shut the door, close the window—were you born in a barn?" said town classmates, and on the playing fields, in derision—"You couldn't hit the broad side of a barn." They invoked barns to disparage, whereas I heard of tramps sleeping in roadside barns and wouldn't have minded doing the same. I loved the drumming of hail or heavy rain on the tin roof (such a pounding by the universe but still I was sheltered!), and the warmth in winter from animal heat; throaty, guttural German sounds from the pigpens; the stately, muffled, fur-coated movements of the cattle; the glow from the dim, cob-webbed windows of the milking section when I stood in snow-banks outside—then going into the barn, catching the lactic smells of mother and babyhood, feeling the calmness of this extraction—gentle milking—the cows hardly aware what was happening.

Those barns were alive because we were; and what was left of Grandfather was hand-hewn beams and whittled oak pegs that bore testimony to his intentions. When he'd viewed miles of tall prairie grass straight to the horizon, enclosing him in a perfect but terrifying circle, he began to build out and up—from the bull's-eye of that circle. I caught his aspiration and faith, but who of us could fulfill what he thought he'd only begun? Not my father, who died young of pneumonia, pre-ceding Grandfather, nor Uncle Jack, who loved machinery not as a means to the usual ends of farming but as a fascination itself; nor his children, nor me—we left.

Now our backward glance is unsullied by actual, daily in-volvement; only Uncle Jack remained home to deal with farm matters. When part of the Lower Barn roof flew away in a tornado, he cursed the immensity of the structure, the difficulty of getting any roofers to come, the awful cost of tin sheeting these days. "Barns can kill you," he told me. He no longer fed Angus herds or even fattened pigs for market (on Social Security, he mustn't earn too much); the barns stood empty in a dreamlike sleep, waiting for the associations of human and animal life to match their inward sense of existence; swallows still glided through open doors and windows, trying to keep the dark enclosures alive. A neighbor offered to rent the hog section for his thoroughbred, pedigreed herd, since no cholera had ever flourished there. Meanwhile, the insurance rates on barns kept rising, the tax assessments, too. The bright vermilion paint had faded to a dried-blood color. Uncle Jack awaited the return of some Indians from the South Sioux City, Nebraska, reservation, who'd stopped by our farm in the 1930's and painted the barns so cheaply. But the years passed and no

Indians showed up. "Where are those Indians?" he'd say every now and then.

At last he tore down the whole north-south section of the Upper Barn, obliterating the Maltese cross, making a conventional one-way barn. Six-by-six beams with their sockets gouged out for end-to-end lapping, like the male/female grooving in carpentry, lay in a stack to be picked up by any farmer who happened to drive into the yard and see them: laid as low and lifeless as Grandfather in his coffin in 1931. Some of those timbers were taken by the neighbors to build a loafing shed for their milch herd—the only sort of barn a modern farmer needs for his cattle. The rest, by rain or snow, would find a way to the earth, decompose into it, eventually making rich humus—a long and final rest after one hundred years' postponement. Is this a loss?

What farmer would say so. Something will grow.

3.   Queen of Hearts

The new teacher, Miss Flock, was hired just one week before country school opened. Through Mother's last-minute influence, two neighbor-children, DeWayne and Orban, who were to attend the Catholic parochial school, enrolled instead in the rural schoolhouse, thus keeping it open one more year. My cousin Lois and I were the last of our family still in the lower grades, and everyone thought it best if we could continue at the one-room schoolhouse three-quarters of a mile away, rather than attend public school in town. As the year developed, I don't know how we could have gotten along without Orban, a first-year scholar, for we taught him to play pinochle, and counting Miss Flock we totaled eight—the right number exactly for a double round.

Because each year was expected to be the last, the schoolhouse had slipped into disrepair and listed to one side over its foundation of cracking limestone. The building was about the size of our corncrib, large and peeling-white, with sparrows' nests straggling from the eaves. A row of wind-stunted box elder and ash trees rimmed the schoolyard, and the plot was moored to the gravel road by a homemade roadway. When a high gale blew off the flat cornfields, the loose shingles fluttered and snapped like the flag we ceremoniously raised aloft each morning and revered with religious awe.

I mention the flag because Miss Crakow, our former teacher, instilled in our imaginations an enormous respect for it. The command never to let the flag touch the ground came to imply that, if it did, the cloth would snarlingly wrap around us. And if it were raised upside down—even halfway—through gross carelessness, doom would descend. In the schoolhouse the flag lay on a shelf in front, flanked by pictures of George Washington and Abraham Lincoln, relics for contemplation. We were patriotic, every one of us. We pledged allegiance each morning in case anyone had had a change of heart overnight. Our hands were over our hearts—and it had to be the correct heart on the left side, or she rapped our knuckles with the ruler. But after many years of teaching, when all of us were certain of her permanence, Miss Crakow got married and left us to shift for our patriotic selves—an almost traitorous act, except that surely she didn't imagine that Miss Flock, when she arrived, would scarcely pay a bit of attention to the Red, White, and Blue.

But then, no one could have anticipated Miss Flock, even the wisest. On the first day her Hupmobile bounced across the ditch over the sunken fill-in and onto the schoolyard just a few minutes before nine o'clock. All seven of us were assembled on the bare, open platform in front of the school door. On this little shelf Miss Crakow had held her miniature military drill, and by this time we would have been all set to watch the flag go up. Now I sat peeling splinters off the porch and sticking them quietly into Delbert, who stupidly complained aloud of wasps. Little Orban, overalled to within an inch of his chin, looked furtively at us and at the locked door to knowledge, while the meadowlarks in the fields sang unending praise.

We silently watched the Hupmobile swish through the bluegrass and come to a gasping halt under the shadiest tree. Miss Flock smiled, climbed out, and slammed the door with verve. "What're you doin' here so early? School starts at nine, and that's about when I'll get here." We all wanted to inform her that Miss Crakow had always arrived an hour early, but none of us said a word. When she marched onto the platform we scattered from her path. "I've got a long ways to come." She took keys from a purse, glittery in the sunshine. "Farther'n you have." She looked directly at Orban. He was too frightened to speak. "What's the matter, can't any of you talk? I learned when I was two and been at it ever since."

She got the door open with the help of a firm kick and walked inside. Desks had been polished, the floor swept with red oily compound, and the curtains laundered. All this had been accomplished by the wives of the school directors—Uncle Jack was on the board. "You there," Miss Flock said as she nabbed DeWayne, who towered a foot above her. "What's your name?" He told her with a lazy smile because he figured he'd have some fun with this one. "How old are you?"

"Prit near sixteen."

"Well, you let me know when you *are*. You're too big to be in school. Don't your dad need you on the farm?"

"He could use me all right," said DeWayne, "but I don't need him."

We all laughed. Miss Flock said, "Since you're the oldest boy in school you're going to do the work. Get the bucket of drinking water from the trunk of my car. And after you've brought it in, scrub the sink and washstand. When it gets cold in fall, I'll have you hauling coal every day. You'll learn something yet in this school."

Miss Flock marched to the front and stood in the morning sunlight. Her dark hair was pulled tightly back off her face and fell without much pretense of curl behind her ears. I thought she was beautiful, at least compared to the last one. Her features were regular, and plenty of them; she would be a good subject for observation in the hundreds of hours that lay ahead, and every little piece of her could be noticed and dissected.

"Take your seats," she announced. Since we had no assigned seats, this was perplexing, but we stirred ourselves to crawl in somewhere and tested the desks for size. We pulled out the resistant drawers, wriggled, rocked, and fingered the hard, squashed gum on the undersides of the desk tops. After considering whether neighbors seemed satisfactory, we made our choices. "Through?" she finally asked, not having paid us the least attention. "All right now, I'm going to read some literature to you before we do anything else. You better shut up and listen because I could just as easy not read."

She picked up the book. "This is *The Bobbsey Twins in South Dakota,* Chapter One. 'On that first morning in the wonderful wheat country, the twins woke up and asked, "Where are we?" ' "

She read on and on, passing Chapters Five and Six. At the end of each section she paused, teasing us, until we applauded to show our interest. Things really became exciting and I hardly heard my stomach growling, a sure sign it was eleven o'clock. "Now this is absolutely the last," she said, launching into the eleventh chapter. I knew it was hard for her to put the book away, for she'd become highly interested in the story; but she read in such a fast singsong we couldn't understand her anymore.

Finally, with an exhausted slam of the book she declared recess and moved quickly for a dipper of water. We played softball until we got so hungry we had to fetch our lunch pails. Miss Flock seemed to take our general declaration of noon hour in stride. We sat on the platform before the front door and dangled our legs over the edge while we munched dry sandwiches and gurgled milk from our vacuum bottles.

Miss Flock had a strange lunch, not in the least balanced. She ate five huge dill pickles right in a row, then a deviled egg and a piece of cream pie that was gooey and difficult to manage. After wiping cream fluff from her nose she asked if anyone would care to finish her coffee. We all spoke, eager to see if it would stunt our growth. Miss Flock smiled and passed her cup around. A rich feeling of excitement and freedom crept over me. I had to share it with Delbert. "She ain't no teacher," I whispered to him. "She's a kid like us."

"I ain't afraid of her," Delbert said, swaggering—missing my point.

I crawled over to Norma. "What do you think of her?"

"She sure ain't like the other one."

"She ain't a teacher," I whispered. "There's been some mistake. But let's not tell anybody."

Norma gave me the look of an accomplice. "Let's play ball again after lunch."

But Miss Flock would have none of it. She marched us inside, wound the Victrola, and we started the music lesson with "Old Dog Tray," followed by "De Camptown Races." Miss Flock joined in, a mezzo-soprano, experimenting a bit with harmony, especially when big DeWayne growled along in deep bass. At the end of a song she burst out laughing and sometimes even clapped. We clapped too, having more fun with the singing business than ever before. "Let's see what all you've got here," she murmured, and went through the whole collection, record by record. I didn't know when I'd sung so much, and Miss Flock, challenged by the vocalists, couldn't seem to stop.

I began to feel a little uneasy lest some parent stop by and wonder if the song fest should take the place of arithmetic and spelling. But of course no parent would visit unless invited, and none of us were driven to school by car, so there was no chance of a parental glimpse into our life there. We walked from our farms even in winter when snowbanks closed the roads; we traveled in a group, gathering neighbors along the way. Miss Flock was in no danger of being checked on unless one of the pupils talked.

Delbert, a stickler for regularity, became increasingly nervous about the neglected flag, which still lay folded neatly on its shelf of honor. At last when a record ended, he marched to the shelf and took up the precious cloth. "Come on, DeWayne, you and me's going to put this up, before it's time soon to take it down."

Miss Flock watched them with lifted eyebrow. "Where they going?" she asked me.

"The flag's supposed to go up in the morning, first thing."

"Well! After this, they'd better not forget it." Then she

slammed shut the Victrola and immediately assigned us lessons. We drew out our books reluctantly, feeling that Delbert's allegiance to rules had spoiled a good thing.

In the middle of the afternoon Miss Flock declared recess and organized another softball game, four against four. She pitched in the balls to DeWayne so hard he complained his hands stung. We could scarcely see the ball, let along bat it. But whenever we did score a hit, she always caught the ball and fired it into first, no matter who was first baseman. I could tell from the way she played that her aim was not just to be a good sport. She loved softball as much as anybody, and we had somehow to live up to her expectations. Otherwise, tomorrow might be different, with endless hours of spelling, geography, and arithmetic.

Although there was no organized conspiracy of silence, each of us guarded the day's events when we went home that night and not a word leaked. It wasn't until later in the year that Miss Flock described the county school superintendent's car and suggested we sound the alarm if it were sighted. As the weather turned colder we stayed indoors more of the time. Someone was assigned to keep an eye on the road—usually the pupil facing the windows across the pinochle table.

Miss Flock was surprised that most of us couldn't play pinochle, for it had been taught her by the time she was five. She looked at little Orban. "No, he ain't too young. He can hold his cards in both hands, and I'll play them. Just so's we have enough people playing to make the melds big."

Miss Flock loved to use two pinochle decks, for then the chances of a double marriage, double pinochle, and a royal straight were infinitely increased. We were dealt quite a mittful, but she said our fingers would get stronger and *that* would be good for us. We let her play Orban's hand until we saw how she could work it to her advantage, and then we insisted everyone should take turns. His hand wasn't useful unless you could make him throw heavy-paying cards on tricks you were about to take. This is what Miss Flock did all the time, and I doubt we would have noticed if little Orban himself hadn't caught on to the game and said suddenly, his eyes watchful and angry, "No, *this* one, *this* one! Not that ten spot!" We were astonished. I looked, and sure enough, Miss Flock had been loading up her tricks until poor Orban had very little left in his hand.

"Don't you have card parties at home?" Miss Flock asked me quickly, to divert attention.

"No," said Lois, who quickly shared Orban's distress. "And little kids wouldn't be allowed to play anyhow."

"Oh, really? I can tell you *I* learned plenty fast. I'd have got a licking if I didn't," she added darkly, and Orban squirmed.

This puzzling reference to her personal life was another bit to add to what we already knew. She'd mentioned attending the local high school two years, for her teaching certificate—ours was her first school. But we wondered if she had any dates or attended dances, and if so, what she wore, for she stuck with tiresome regularity to a shapeless purple dress. Since neighborhood card parties were the only social life she mentioned, I thought a clan of card players met almost every night. At home I guardedly asked why we didn't belong to such a group, and their objection was that Catholics and Protestants were all mixed up at card parties. With kids along associating with one another, likely as not the Catholics would grab off a few Protestants through marriage, and *that* would be the upshot of all the card playing. I figured maybe Miss Flock didn't have the Catholic problem we had.

In late October, DeWayne turned sixteen, and though he could have legally quit school, Miss Flock persuaded him to stay because she wanted him to play father in the Christmas pageant. Our school Christmas programs in the past had not been elaborate, but clearly Miss Flock had other ideas. Pinochle sessions were cut short in November and soon after lunch we'd drag the teacher's desk behind the stove, shove the recitation bench along the opposite wall, and walk on stage. Orban, Lois, and I pretended to be children, and Norma played the mother with a vengeance rivaled only by Norma's mother. Miss Flock made up the lines as we went along and we were supposed to remember them.

Occasionally we studied. In a burst of sudden academic enthusiasm, Miss Flock sent us to our books. As though it were all a game, we'd rush through recitations, have spelling bees, and hop up and down from our seats to try our minds at learning. But play rehearsals dominated the days, and after a few weeks of constant practice, we knew our "speeches" perfectly. Then Miss Flock worried lest we forget the play before Christmas arrived. To sustain our interest, we embarked upon an ambitious project of making hand-decorated invitations for all parents and members of the school board. Each adorned card was to be different, in as many colors as possible, with extensive use of gold and silver dust, which Miss Flock valued so highly that she kept the vials in her purse at all times.

Once the invitations were completed, she suggested we make Christmas presents for our parents. After several abortive attempts at fancy hot pads, book ends, and lamp shades, we settled down to vary a basic idea supplied by Miss Flock—we painted doorstops. The raw material was a good-sized stone. Although some of us came from the same family, Miss Flock maintained that two stones or even three could be useful around the house for keeping doors open, or possibly forcing them shut. Now, in this section of Iowa stones were about as rare as cactuses, and when a farmer turned one up, neighbors crossed the fields to look it over. The only place we knew there were stones was under our schoolhouse—the foundation, and so we hauled away all likely-looking chunks. "Not near the corners," warned Miss Flock. "Don't mess around with *those* stones. We need something to hold the building up."

When processing the stones, Miss Flock was in doubt about what to try first. We used up all the drinking water in washing the rocks, then placed them in the sun to dry on the front platform. Several of us varnished them. DeWayne insisted on painting designs, which ran together until he had a mess that looked like something a huge bird had emitted in mulberry season. Norma and Delbert were probably on the right track, for they clipped out pieces of colored construction paper and slapped them in patterns onto their rocks, hoping to make a decal which could be covered with varnish. But they ran into chemical difficulties, having applied the varnish when the stones were still wet. The result, when it dried, was a monstrous, ragged oddity that defied explanation, even though there were two of them. Miss Flock thought they were wonderfully funny, and when we all got through laughing, Norma confessed that her stone wouldn't even do for knocking mud from your overshoes. Finally, with a joyous shout we gave up, piled all our stones together in a cairn on the workbench, and sat down for a good game of pinochle.

In the weeks preceding the Christmas pageant we played cards every chance we could, "to relax us," said Miss Flock. We decorated the schoolroom with fringed crepe paper streamers and pinned cutouts of stars and Christmas trees to the window curtains. On the day of the performance, the last afternoon before vacation, Miss Flock brought homemade cookies and pots of coffee. The audience arrived well ahead of time, and from behind the bed sheets strung across the stage we watched them squeezing into our desks—like ridiculous, overgrown children. Then our pageant began, and never had we given such a performance. In an emotional scene Norma wept so copiously she alarmed the cast and several mothers seemed about to rush forward. As the curtains closed the applause was tremendous.

Presents were passed around and Miss Flock collected a handsome pile, gifts from each of us and from all the parents. It was clearly her day; everyone in the audience felt moved to tell her how talented she was with children and how in all the years of the country school there'd never been a Christmas program as good as this.

"Having the right teacher, the first years," I heard Mother say, "is *so* important!" She'd taught country school herself before marriage; she looked dotingly at Miss Flock. I thought how upset she and everyone would be if they knew the truth. *Why didn't you tell us?* they'd ask. But I could never explain our conspiracy. I just knew I'd never betray Miss Flock and I was sure none of us would.

However, on the way home, Orban, who was riding with us,

blurted out, "Why are the eights no good when you play pinochle?"

DeWayne jabbed him in the ribs. "Because that's the game, stupid."

A pheasant whirred out of the snowy ditch in burnished glory, and Mother and Aunt Lizzie cried, "Oh, look at him!"

"Well, I'm tired of pinochle," said Orban.

"Nobody's saying you'll ever have to play it," his mother replied.

"That's what *you* think!" Orban tried to say more, but DeWayne throttled him, and just then we drove into their farmyard—and let them out. In the farewells, DeWayne's mother said, "You know, I said to DeWayne, 'You're sixteen now and you don't *have* to go up to school no more.' But you know what he says to me? 'Mom, I *want* to keep it up.'"

"A good teacher makes *all* the difference," said Mother.

4. Rooms of the House

A pelican stuffed with sawdust was in the attic. We'd ride the humped, feathered back as if it were an ostrich, stare at the yellow glass eyes and stroke the lizard-skin pouch under the beak, not finding plump fish there, only shifting granular wood pulp, like in the limbs of dolls—stuff of no life. Rigid fowl legs rose above the huge webbed feet, which were immured in varnish and stuck to a wooden platform. We'd fall over, screaming, the bird on top of us, ocher beak pecking the attic floor.

What are you kids doing up there?

Playing. Rain pounded the tin roof and washed the small-paned windows, making such a tropical noise we almost forgot our life below on the Iowa farm. We were living in the fabulous tree house of the family past, enchanted by these talismans of other lives, earlier existences. The pelican stood at the head of the stairs under a cloth cover, so that his white feathers wouldn't gray any further. My father had shot him years before in response to a neighbor's phone call: *Come quick, Henry, a strange bird's sitting on our barn roof.* Nobody had ever seen such a queer-looking creature—who'd believe it? Simply perched there without moving. Father's rifle shot brought it down and the taxidermist hid the spot where the bullet entered; we could never find the pucker. Father succumbed not long afterward, and no further information was given as to how the pelican came to be in our attic. Nor were other animals, fish, or birds mounted, perhaps because no game as unusual appeared—or, more likely, once the pelican entered our household, it became clear there was nothing to do with the thing except put it away, as we stashed memorabilia of earlier lives upstairs without having to commit a decision of value. Nowadays our own lives are stored there: schoolbooks and A-marked examination papers, report cards, letters home, newspaper clippings about our far-off doings, boots, clothes, and pennants. Stuffing dead as sawdust.

But how had a pelican flown into Iowa? Our teachers scolded us for telling fibs when we bragged about what we had at home. Time and again one of us had to carry the pelican into the classroom. We learned of the seasonal migration of birds along flyways, high over rivers, and how storms sometimes threw off even the best bird navigators. In early October we'd wake in the middle of a moonlit night to the high honking of Canadian geese on their route south. Something strange had happened to this pelican, confusing him. I brooded over the lesson we were to absorb from this bird trophy, particularly since it represented a conspicuous, dramatic act by my now nonexistent and untalked-about father. The glassy yellow eyes with black pupils alerted us: none must shoot a pelican, under penalty of death.

Lives of the dead became active in the attic. Without this inquisitive, rainy-day scurrying, they'd never lift up out of the detritus of the past. And yet, Grandma's spinning wheel was merely the authentic implement it appeared to be; she alone knew how to use it but wasn't interested. Our parents treasured the spinning wheel as a genuine antique, but we couldn't mingle our lives with it, somehow, and preferred the leftovers of earlier days whose identities or purposes were less clear, whose presence in the attic had been forgotten—like the Montgomery Ward mahogany love seat and chair of my grandparents. The green plush cushions and high-curved, uncomfortable backs weren't modern in appearance, the furniture not good enough to be taken to town when Grandfather retired; too old-fashioned for my parents or Uncle Jack and Aunt Lizzie to want downstairs in the parlor. The same was true of the foot-pedal organ, bellows rather wheezy, which we'd work until exhausting ourselves, playing eerie, made-up tunes in a minor key. And Mother's trunk, containing stiff, high-heeled party shoes, Father's twenty-dollar silk shirts, bank statements for the years between 1910 and 1928, and *Light on Dark Corners,* a bride's handbook on what to expect when her husband demanded his marital rights. Mother's curling irons and nail buffers suggested that once she became a widow her life had largely been put away into this trunk, all the married part of it at least.

We excavated cardboard cartons filled with hard old shoes—couldn't give them to the Salvation Army if you tried. Since our trash piles in the grove were filling up too fast with tin cans and bottles, we carefully burned what could be consumed and served the pigs all edible garbage, but many of our discards couldn't be disposed of except in the attic, which finally became a kind of dump. Poles strung along the rafters supported garment bags with glassine windows, for all the coats, dresses, and suits not currently in use but possibly wanted by one of us, someday. Here under the roof we kept iron beds and springs, disassembled and stacked; broken chairs, chamber pots, chipped-veneer dressers with murky mirrors, empty dish barrels, used wrapping paper, cribs, playpens, old toys, copies of *The National Geographic, Life, Collier's,* boxes of textbooks, novels by Winston Churchill, and a year's supply of toilet paper. In the musty, secret air of the attic, delving into the family rag bag, we sneezed from the dust of our burrowings and drifted in fine, imaginary journeys.

Mother and Aunt Lizzie disapproved of our investigations, saying we messed up what was already a burden of bad housekeeping to their minds. Someday they always meant to "straighten out the attic," mop, scrub, and throw away the old stuff (*some*place else)—but it was the one part of the house they simply never got to. We'd emerge from the attic darkness blinking, guiltily shedding our make-believe world, which had accomplished nothing and merely wasted time, knowing we'd done something not quite approved of but never actually defined. When we pulled on the funny old clothes and stepped into the awful hobo shoes, weren't we making fun of people and times past that deserved some respect? Yes, but more seriously, what was the point of such mooning and dreaming?

Uncle Jack knew that our dilatory attic life might weaken our abilities, rendering us incapable of accomplishing much. If he happened to catch us frittering away our time playing with the past, we felt his large-limbed disapproval, his reality in the living moment of today. Coming up the attic stairs, his two-hundred-twenty-pound hulk dissipated the magic air. Although his World War gear adorned the north wing window and his castoffs mingled with other people's here, his trips to the attic were never for getting in touch with dead associations. He was always on urgent business: checking the enormous tank under the eaves (our water pressure system) to see that it was filling properly from the basement pump, or mending a broken windowpane or assembling a needed bed. He even suggested a convenient use for the lofty attic space—why didn't we dry out our bittersweet bouquets up here? When they were cured, hanging heads-down from their stems, we could easily collect them for our display spot in Aunt Bertha's hat shop, to be sold at twenty-five cents a bunch.

Under the tin roof the attic was a climate of extreme temperatures: broiling hot in summer but quickly cool when wet with dew; in winter the house heat rose to the top, infiltrating the chill. Never was all of the attic explored, not way back to the unfinished floor at the eaves where the roof lay on top of the joists. There was always the possibility of finding some forgotten trunk or misplaced Christmas presents (Santa Claus arrived by way of the attic, and when we were supposed to be sleeping, Christmas Eve, we'd hear the soft creak of the attic door hinges and much tiptoeing in the hall). The attic and basement were the only areas of the house that remained what they were throughout the years. All other rooms underwent transformations as startling as our own developing lives: for this was how we used the house.

At various times I slept in every bedroom. While an infant, I inhabited the large master bedroom on the second floor, where my parents slept and my widowed mother remained; and when I was deemed too old to be in the same room with her, my sister became the occupant and I moved to the "boys' room," cots lined up in a dormitory row. The choicest bedroom on the second floor was just outside the attic door, windows looking out upon the grove. Catching chicken pox first placed me there in quarantine, with a toy telegraph set rigged up, wires leading to the kitchen; I could tap out my desires and demands for anyone on the other end to decode, if they deigned to. But I wasn't allowed to live there long, for others wanted it and had more seniority, or better arguments: "A girl should have a room to herself," claimed my sister. When Barney, the hired man, married and left, we greedily eyed his quarters above the kitchen, painted the place light blue, put in a radiator, and two of us boys moved in. But roommates were always changing, due to our flexible attitude toward the resources this house offered, and there was little quarreling among us since nobody's room situation was permanent.

On an upstairs bedroom windowpane, Aunt Anne had scratched her name with a diamond soon after that wing of the house was built. *Anna,* she called herself then, a name bearing long dresses and a scent of lavender. The closet with its old-fashioned floral wallpaper had sheltered her clothes—a small room content with its darkness when the door was shut, a good place for her to hide from Grandfather's wrath when she'd been bad. We painted the walls of this room pastel purple with a "decorator's" line of paint just under the ceiling in a darker shade; we asserted our contemporary importance in this chamber, yet left the highly varnished, gleaming woodwork alone, for Grandfather had meant the wood to show. Above every room door was a transom for proper ventilation, to let in the odors of coffee and baking bread, the distant sounds of family somewhere in the house; in the night, children early-to-bed, sleepily saw the transom glowing, a comforting reminder that a parent wasn't far away.

When we were most numerous, filling every corner of the building, only two rooms downstairs were public family rooms: the kitchen and "dining room," which, since all but company meals were eaten in the kitchen, was actually our living room. Under the stamped-tin dining-room ceiling, intricate in design as a metal carpet, hung a chandelier like an opaque punchbowl with pendent globes at the rim. Winter evenings we'd sit around the table as Lizzie read aloud from *Heidi* or *Swiss Family Robinson*. With her expressive, forensic talents, she could catch the inflections and project the personalities of the characters lingering in the pages. She suffered from eye strain, however, perhaps from the tried-on-in-the-dime-store glasses, and though her head ached, we were relentless in our request to have *her* read, not someone else.

A small master bedroom on the dark, north side of the house was a fine retreat from the ever-brilliant prairie light—a farmer's den for repose, here the elements wouldn't prod him. Since our grove was thick with evergreens, even in winter the north wind was no menace, and birds on the feeders provided civilized entertainment. Located on the first floor, this bedroom had a chain-and-pulley device in the closet, which was directly over the furnace, so that on winter nights one could regulate the damper without a trip to the basement. Though small in size, probably fifteen by twelve feet, the room contained five burled-pine doors. The madness of so many openings unsettled me, obsessed me, when I lived there. Grandfather's architectural talents had encountered some sort of insolvable problem. One door led to the hall and family rooms; another was the closet with the furnace device; then, a wall space wide enough for a dresser, but next to *that* was a door opening onto a three-cornered little space of no possible use—clearly a mistake covered up by beautiful woodwork. A fourth door opened to a walk-in closet where we stored extra table leaves and the vacuum cleaner but kept the floor clear so that we could lift up the heavy trap door and descend the ladder-stairs to the basement. For a child sleeping in this chamber, aware of the sinister possibilities of Poe and Stevenson trap doors, *this* was the closet to keep a careful eye on. A fifth door, usually locked and eventually sealed, led to the old-time parlor, since converted into a bedroom. Like an Oriental potentate whose honor demanded first-access through a portal, Grandfather had doors leading to every important part of the house.

Porches were the intermediate stations between earth and home, and our house had as many porches as decks on a ship. In addition to the wrap-around, screened-in front porch, there was a small kitchen porch with a southern exposure—a good place to draw on boots and where the cats and dog sunned themselves in chilly weather. A north porch, largely enclosed, also gave off from the kitchen, like a spare room that almost got away to the outdoors. Here we stored old newspapers and magazines, kept canned goods soon to be consumed, empty bottles waiting to be returned, cleaning mops, rags, bushel baskets of cobs and stacks of wood for the cookstove, and in the years before the Frigidaire the kerosene refrigerator, with its oily smells and throaty rumbles. A heated porch (not quite a bona fide house room) was just outside the dining room and always called "the washroom." We stashed outer coats and rubbers there and the men scrubbed themselves at the big sink with harsh, gritty bars of scouring soap. Razor strops swung menacingly from the coat hooks, for the room was large enough for Jack to whip his bad boys, and although I was spared these scourgings, I heard the yowls from the older ones and the sharp leather cracks as they "got a licking." This was Jack's room.

The basement, counterpart of the attic, was rich in the fringe-matter of our life. Just inside the cellar door Jack had set up a lathe for winter night woodworking and a bench for performing household repairs. On this lathe I dowled out a lamp base and bulbous legs for attaching to a coffee table. Older brothers made furniture in school "shop" classes: a plant stand for Lizzie's begonias, an oak bedroom dresser and chest of drawers, a magazine scuttle, end tables, chairs. In the vise we'd crack black walnuts and spend hours digging out the oily, pungent meats. Monday washings were accomplished in this same basement room, and in summer I'd help Lizzie run clothes through the wringer, carry heavy baskets of wet laundry upstairs to the clotheslines strung between trees and buildings. I'd drain the dirty wash water and clean up (allowed to keep all coins caught in the sieve trap), and if our abandoned-well septic tank system in the grove wasn't taking it all, Uncle Jack would round up his crew and we'd haul the smelly buckets out of the hole in the ground and dump the sewage into a nearby field, where enormous corn would grow the following year. Lizzie's laundry soap consisted of animal fat, glycerin, and lye, which she made each year; the firm, tallow-looking soap would suds up well, but we never used it elsewhere in the house.

We stored eggs in the basement each day, sorting them from egg bucket to crate and candled them if necessary against the tool-bench light bulb. The unsuitable-for-sale eggs, blood-stained, misshapen, cracked, were set aside for our immediate kitchen use. Lizzie's "sloppy pancakes," a kind of crêpe, consisted almost entirely of eggs, and we had them for breakfast three or four mornings a week. The hen's preservative was destroyed in washing eggs, so our consumption had to be accomplished quickly to prevent waste. Should an egg be suspected of overage, we'd set it aside for the daily mess of cats' scrambled eggs. We loved the story of the tramp in the chicken barn stealing eggs for his meal, cracking them above his head and drinking them down—and how, after one crack, *cheep, cheep,* said the chick; and the tramp: "You spoke too late!"

In a crude basement room which looked as if it had been blasted out of the earth our bullets were manufactured. A light bulb dangled over a workbench where Jack kept his rows of empty cartridges, bags of shot, bottles of powder, strips of caps—and file, tamper, and bowl for melting wax to hold the bullet in position. He chiefly fabricated rifle and pistol bullets, replacing the caps and filling the metal containers, for the cardboard casings of shotgun shells had to be purchased and hence the saving wasn't so great. We weren't allowed to step over the high barrier into this cave unless Jack sat at his bench making bullets. What confidence the sight of him there instilled in us! Upstairs we might play gang war with spring-powered toy pistols that shot sucker sticks with suction cups on the end (they'd land *plock* on any flat target and leave a red kiss-mark of death on a victim's arm, forehead, neck), but down here the real family firepower was being quietly amassed. In these Depression years of bank robbers, gypsies, tramps, kid-napers, cattle rustlers, and chicken thieves, our farm bristled with guns like a fort, possessed an army of kids to aid in defense and a magazine room of ammunition.

Like the attic, the basement was tantalizingly beyond total scrutiny: one never got to the end of discoveries—jars of pre-served fruits from who knew what season in a cobwebbed, forgotten corner, old beehive racks, dim, enormous crocks. There was never quite enough light from the dirty cellar windows or the weak-watted bulb to see all that a room might contain under the rows of obscuring shelves. In February the potato cellar was a jungly mass of greenish-yellow sprouts, smelling funky as armpits, a whole mound of irrepressible life which would never make it out of the cellar.

Since we had no genuine cave or dugout, the basement was our tornado emergency cellar, for although a twister might lift the entire house like a hat from our heads, we'd be un-touched in our hole. We were instructed in tornado safety as we were in dealing with fire, farm animals, machinery. Should a tornado sweep across the prairie while we were walking the exposed mile to school, black tail weaving drunkenly across the fields like the Palmer-method swirls which we made in pen-manship class, lifting cornstalks, animals, barns to the top of its funnel, we were told to plunge into the nearest ditch and, better yet, crawl into a culvert if any were nearby. Join the earth, flatten one's flesh full length along it, cling to plant roots.

Tornadoes usually developed in late afternoon from a westerly direction. We'd descend to the cellar and cluster along the west wall, since the house, if it were carried off, would move up and

away from us. Because the dense grove limited our view of
the twister, we'd rely upon Jack's reports, from his scrutiny
of the sky on the open lawn, and peer out the cellar windows
to see the thrashing trees—particularly "Aunt Anne's oak,"
which she'd planted as a seedling in the 1880's, now our
biggest tree. It survived all the storms, but the cottonwoods
tumbled like balsa in the high winds. Occasionally in the middle
of the night we'd be roused from bed by an urgent parent:
"Bad storm coming—we're going to the cellar!" Stabbed awake
by the awful words, we'd leap from the sheets, hurry into
shoes or slippers, and descend to the basement via the inside
route, through the trap door. Down there in the clammy dark,
I'd think of the empty, window-eyed rooms blinking at the
flashes of lightning, witnessing the roiled clouds. After the rain
was safely pouring down, the wind blown over, we'd crawl
upstairs—how exceedingly empty the rooms seemed! As we
grew older we scoffed at the alarmist cellar dives, for the
neighbor-children lived more dangerously and seldom took such
precautions. No twister touched our buildings or grove, and
yet every year we saw devasting paths chewed through nearby
cornfields, and once even the town was hit.

While the attic stored the family dead things, the basement
kept everything alive—all those rows of garden produce still
edible and waiting in jars for our hunger to catch up with
them; wood from the grove and coal to feed the furnace;
potatoes, onions, turnips, carrots smelling of earth and life,
pungent as sperm. Here in these basement chambers in February,
during the false thaw not long after Groundhog Day, we did
the family butchering. The actual slaughtering took place in
the barns, beef and pig carcasses hung on meathooks from
the hay loader. On those days of melting snow it was just
cool enough to preserve the meat, yet comfortably warm enough
for the men to scald hides, scrape bristles, eviscerate the critters
—saving livers, hearts, brains, and other usable parts—quarter
the rest, to be further carved into steaks, roasts, and chops on
basement trestle tables. The semicool cellar rooms were perfect

for sausage-making and preparation of bacon and hams, which were placed in brine before the smokehouse was fired up.

Aunt Bertha let her partner run the hat shop these days and along with Grandma arrived on the farm to help out. Blond and blue-eyed, Bertha was still a pretty *Mädchen* with a cheering, irrepressible energy. She was dressed in her butcher's outfit; layers of tattered, dark woolen skirts and sweaters, rags compared to her usual stylish outfits. She and her mother had left the country life in 1919, but they'd not gone far and kept refreshing themselves with year-round provender from the farm, never having divested themselves of the idea that the farm wasn't theirs, partly because they still owned a piece of it. Since Grandfather's estate settlement was always postponed, Jack paid rent on Grandma's widow portion in whatever amount he thought appropriate. Although the value of livestock and machinery had been accounted for in the deal whereby Father and Jack came to manage the farm, the chickens had been totally forgotten. For years afterward Bertha regarded our flock as "Ma's chickens," umpteen generations after the original ones—eggs and as many fryers as needed were shamelessly expected from us.

Grandma very rarely returned to the farm. Even in her retirement house she seemed remote in her quiet privacy, spoke in a cracked voice on neutral topics such as the weather or crops, her eyes uneasy behind the thick lenses—sometimes suddenly and frighteningly magnified by the glass. Among her offspring she spoke a lively Low German, lilting with laughter —she became a different person. Even though she'd been born in Iowa and lived like an American for eighty years, her life was encased in the foreign language; she was sealed off from us. Of course she knew English but in her later years preferred German—she was reeling backward while we were moving forward. We assumed she'd forgotten what it was like to be as young as we were, but instead, she must have been gazing in perplexity at these grandchildren so thoroughly Americanized they didn't even know the language of their forebears.

Butchering time reminded her of the old days. She'd come

out to the farm with Aunt Bertha, her dress reaching all the
way to her black, solid shoes, on her gray-white head a small
bonnet with a fringe of ruffle around it, like the mobcaps of
the eighteenth century. She knew all about sausage-making
and was the only one who could produce blood pudding; she
was needed and that's why she came. The meat grinder screwed
to the basement table would spew out worms of pork—then
came the kneading and spicing, "throw in more pepper, Bert,"
from Grandma to her daughter, sowing herbs into the red
flesh like broadcasting oats upon a field. Finally all the in-
gredients were dumped into the black iron sausage press.
Meanwhile, upstairs Lizzie fired up boilers of water on the
kitchen stove, for sterilizing jars in which the sausages would
be canned. Pans of blood sat on the oak kitchen table and
cabinet shelves, waiting for Grandma. Her batches of blood
pudding always came out an inch high with gobs of suet here
and there—and was cut into squares like brownies.

Aunt Bertha would attach the slimy sausage casing to the
press spout while one of us turned the big handle. The pig's
intestines had been carefully washed in a saline solution, and
now the sausage meat oozed out the nozzle and filled the opaque
sleeve. When the right extension was achieved, she'd make a
deft knot and start another. The sausages to be cooked in jars
would be later placed upon shelves in the far cellar rooms;
when these were opened and the meat browned in a frying
pan, the wrinkly skins of the sausages would come away from
the insides as easily as one pulled off healed sunburn. Other
sausages were packed in lard in huge white crocks, and many
were strung from the rafters of the smokehouse to be cured.

In the cottonwood grove, among chokecherry clumps and
small timber, our smokehouse shack looked as nibbled as a
gingerbread house. Some of the moss-covered shingles were
missing; loose siding and knotholes allowed the drift of blue
smoke, as if the place were on fire, such drainage necessary
for the flow of smoke to pass the hams, bacon, and sausages
strung on twine from the rafters, like saddles. Jack constructed
his cave man's bonfire in the earthen floor, a little teepee of

hickory, apple, or walnut firewood—he'd try different woods and compare results.

Bloodwurst and liverwurst were highly prized among us, but my favorite was the purply, pungent lung sausage, strong in smoke taste. I tried to forget it was made of pigs' lungs and revolting innards. The foremost family pride in wurst was Jack's summer sausage, a recipe from Grandma and "the old days," comprised of raw pork and various spices, smoke-cured for many weeks. Before we were aware of the dangers of trichinosis, we blithely ate summer sausage throughout the year, serving it as a delicacy to all guests. Later for safety's sake we sent a sample each spring to Ames for analysis, thinking how lucky that university lab technician was—to have a chance to taste such sausage—and of course our product was never found tainted.

I came to revel in the butcher's challenging aim of making palatable what would ordinarily seem inutile parts of an animal. I liked headcheese and tripe, also pigs' feet, tails, and ears—which were pickled in vinegar and served in little china boats. I developed a public craving for pigs' tails especially (mostly to be different), and my elders laughed in Teutonic approval as I nibbled away on the vertebrae, each joint getting a little smaller. If I stopped to think about what I was doing, I'd become disgusted and taste nothing but gristly vinegar. But I professed to crave tails passionately, and the remains would lie coiled on my plate, reminding me of rats' tails, bones white and delicately jointed. Looking hard, I might see Grandma's fingers lying there, long and lean, as she dug into bowls of ground pork, mixing sage, salt, and pepper, the meat as cold as her fingers—lumbering slowly in the raw mash, bone and flesh trying to become one again.

We committed so much of ourselves to the rooms of the house while we lived there that a presence seemed to cling long after all of us had gone. Years later walking up the familiar attic steps, I felt the wash of family beings almost palpable on face and body—I was swimming in the congealed and unreleased atmosphere of those years of rooms. The pelican no longer presided in the attic: donated to the science department of the high school by the last of us who was a pupil there. Most everything else remained and what was to be done with it? I felt buried by the overlay and scrambled to dispose of my own leavings—hauled out school themes, books, letters, high school newspapers, and burned them in the orchard barrel used for such purposes. While stirring the charred sheets, I noticed the ever-present stand of American Beauty roses, which we'd always called "the ash pile roses" and which had actually been planted by Aunt Mary, Father's sister, who'd died years before I was born. The living presence of these flowers seemed to mock my puny efforts to destroy the past. Nor could the rooms be stripped and divested of their associations as long as my eyes looked at them, for rooms held onto existence longer than people did and chambered the inmost reaches of memory.

5. The Milky Way

Molly and Dolly, our Holstein milch cows, were purchased when calves from the Zuckermans, who lived on a run-down farm six miles away. They were the kind of people who opened the pen bars and allowed the animal kingdom leeway everywhere: chickens in the pantry and pigs on the front porch. They'd shamefully let go (which bewildered the livestock) and wallowed in their farm existence without a semblance of control—going under financially as well as morally. Molly and Dolly became pregnant amazingly early, when barely out of heiferhood, for the bull attended to the virgins first. Nine months later when they calved, at nearly the same time, their huge udders went into operation for our siphoned-off benefit. We drank whole milk, while their calves only got thin, blue skimmed milk with suds that disappeared at the touch of a muzzle. Poor, deceived, baby-innocent creatures, with their quick-to-suck mouths, sexually taking our fingers before we knew what they were up to and wanted. We pulled our hands away quickly, out of the tickling, sucking hole of their ardent lips and tongue. No, it was no use; we'd drunk their milk and it couldn't leak from our fingertips. Nothing but wheyish stuff in the trough for them.

For a long time the two Holsteins seemed outsiders. White and black splotched, they looked racially out of keeping with our Aberdeen-Angus herd, velvet dark in the green fields. Molly's black territories were the mass of Asia, while Dolly was more South American, with great seas of white surrounding the black continent. Unlike the Angus herd, which was raised for the beef market in Sioux City, Holsteins were strictly for milking. They invariably produced black calves with never more than a trace of white hair here and there on forehead or flank. They submitted to the domination of Angus-hood, just as Mother and Aunt Lizzie, of Danish and Swiss ancestry with a strain of redhead in their genes, in the seven of us children had produced German-named offspring, all with male line black hair. On a farm it was always the male over the female.

The polled bull, referred to with respect by the women of our household as "the Gentleman," prowled among his twenty or thirty cows with watchful, ophthalmic eyes. His bag of generative power swung heavily between his rear legs, as if it hardly belonged there, for the steers in the barn lots all had been castrated and had no such encumbrances. We children kept on the other side of the fence from the bull, knowing his jealous, flare-up ways, and the lore about the color red— carefully tucking any scarlet bandanna deep into a pocket. With his great boxer's shoulders and that swinging rear pouch, hanging from him like a puncher's bag, the bull seemed a slightly ridiculous figure, maybe because he had nothing to do except mount his females, whereas the cows were busy eating to feed the fetus inside, calving, then producing milk—all a great show of useful activity. And never did the bull seem sillier than when he heaved himself with great effort and got his crushing hoofs on the back of a standing-there-patiently brood cow. The coupling was so improbable—what happened to her tail? And how was he able to aim with that raw red glistening organ? But funniest of all, when the cow tired of the bull's weight she simply walked off, taking the Gentleman in a hobble after her, tottering on his two back legs, helplessly caught in there by his "screw" (which often happened to the boar, too), until finally from the pain of it he'd be shriveled enough to fall out, dribbling sperm that looked from a distance exactly like milk.

The Angus herd cows were allowed to let their calves suck and grow up with all the other field cattle nearby, if their teats were small and uninteresting for our milking industry. But those cows whose bags indicated they might be good milk producers for the next month or so were ushered quickly, along with the Holsteins, into the regular milking operation. Their calves were penned up. Skittery at first and unfamiliar with the whole business, these Angus cows had to be clamped securely into the stanchion, rear legs locked with kicking-chains. There was nothing they could do but submit, though in terror—or revenge—they usually held back their milk amazingly well. At last the silage in the bin became of interest, and as they nibbled the novel milch cow food they let go down below and the milk flowed. Their black, coiled-wool offspring, sequestered in the calf pen along with the other calves of milch cows, like children in boarding school, were made to endure the deprivation of parental love. When the fresh cow's production began to peter out, to perhaps only a third of a five-gallon pail, the trouble wasn't worth it, and this temporary milch cow was released to the field herd again, where every youngster pounced upon her bag for its still-flowing juices.

Sometimes the cow's calf joined her at this time, but the family reunion had come too late for a salving of affection's loss. Indifference had already set in on both sides. Thus the process of life seemed to be a training to survive without the bounty Nature intended, for Her plans were always the rudimentary ones, and if one lapsed into the lull of Her all-encompassing embrace, there'd be no getting out. We'd never grow beyond affection's smother, never be able to survive beyond our homestead gates. We aspired to rise above this insidious pull, and to do so meant accepting deprivation like those calves in the calf pen. We had to harden our sensibilities in order to achieve independence.

From the beginning, Molly looked more like Mother to me

than Dolly, who was her sister, too, just as Aunt Lizzie was
Mother's and both served in the same household. In the alleyway of the manger I'd watch them chew silage—dried-up
corncob bits and chopped kernels, preserved cornstalks still
richly smelling of September fields—while a tremendous milking was going on at their rears. Their bones were mammoth
and tented their hides. They were built like the women in
our family, and I liked their breasts, too, especially Molly's,
which was always bigger than her sister's. The men proudly
said her udders would fill a bushel basket, and they'd grab
hold of a tit—not thumb size but a handful, like the men's
cocks when they pissed against a barn wall. They'd stroke
the nozzle and pull it down for the stream of milk, which
came in a hard, jet force. Sometimes for fun they'd satisfy
the mewling cats and spray in their direction. Frantic and wild
in the milk storm, the cats would half-shut their eyes, lay back
their ears, and open wide their pink triangular mouths, never
minding how much was missed and bonus-landed in their fur,
for they'd spend a delicious after-hour cleaning themselves.
The cow tits in the hands of a skillful milker could hit any
bull's-eye. Did I want a shot of it too? Teasing—the flesh-
colored tube cocked in my direction. No, no—I'd scamper
away, hop onto the laddered sides of the calf pen.

Every faucet on Molly worked; the milker tugged and
squeezed first one set of tits, then another, so that no one
mammary gland was emptied entirely before the others but
all tapered down to mere driblets. In the final stripping, the
tit was slack-skinned and looked almost like the sausage casings
before they were filled by the screw press. The milkers handled
Molly's bag roughly to get every drop they could. Her silky
udder, silvery-white hairs over pink skin, had big bluish veins
that bulged out a little, like Mother's varicose-veined legs.
Her breasts looked as if they should be treated tenderly, but
even the calves when they got a chance to suck angrily butted
into her bag, getting even with the mother for having allowed
them to be cheated of their milk—in the place they knew hurt.

Dolly was slightly smaller, thinner, less placid—at times

restive, nervous. She never allowed the men or boys to become completely familiar with her private parts but always reserved the dignity of independence—no matter what they did to her. An occasional sharp slap from her tail seemed perhaps not intended to whisk flies from her Appalachian back, but to land on the milker's head—as it had. Dolly's tits were not all in working order; one little nubbin near the back was dormant as the nipple on a man's chest. Just after she calved, she came in as good as Molly ever did, however, and among the milkers —Uncle Jack, the older boys, and the hired man—Dolly had her partisans.

These cows kept producing calves and milk, year after year. No matter how many pitchers we drank, how many bowls of Post Toasties and cream we consumed, the flow kept coming. They always passed their TB tests and earned the prized metal clips in their ears, just as we were rewarded in school for A-papers with gummed-label turkeys or Santa Clauses. Never guilty of mischief such as slipping through fence holes into wrong fields, they always stood near the sliding barn door when it was milking time in morning and evening. And when the door rumbled open, they leapt over the sill, udders dragging, without having to be flicked on the rear with a crop or nipped by a herd dog. They were as much a part of our family as the collie dog, Laddie, or the various named cats, and we hated to think of the day when they'd have to be disposed of—sold off. Perhaps they'd just die of old age, carted away by the rendering works truck. Possibly, I thought, we'd always have part of them with us, for once, years before I was born, Father had so loved a Holstein that when he had to ship her to market he arranged for her hide to be treated at the tanning factory, backed with green felt. We used the heavy black and white cover as a car lap robe; under such a wrap it was like being inside the old cow herself.

Evenings at dusk the milkers brought the five-gallon pails in a stately gait (foam on top slipping like islands, trembling, back and forth) to the "washroom," where our cream separator was set up. The pails were so heavy the arm veins of the carriers were distended, like the veins in udders. One whole pail could be poured into the bulbous tank of the separator, then placed empty under the spout where the skimmed milk would come. A small cream can caught the other spout. It was easy, turning the loose wooden handle of the metal arm; round and round as the milk passed through filter papers and into the chamber where it was spun free of its cream. The very last chore a man had to do was take the skimmed milk outside, dump a little into the cats' pan, and bring the rest to the dark calf-barn, where the black calves were waiting, eyes marbled, glazed with excitement, lips blue—hairy mouths like bullheads. Sometimes the fattening shoats would share in the bounty of skimmed milk, and late at night the rats crept out to lick the very last traces from the troughs.

Cream to be sold at the Farmers' Elevator Co-op was stored in the Frigidaire until enough had accumulated. We dipped into the can for cream to drown our oatmeal or dry cereal, lighten our coffee, or coat chocolate and tapioca puddings. Mother cooked custards with caramel undersides—and made the mysterious rennet, a skimmed milk pudding which set from the action of the prepared inner membrane of a calf's stomach, and which we ate with an island of crab apple jelly shimmering in the center of each dish. Aunt Lizzie whipped up lathery cream in a small aluminum canister fitted with two beaters. When ladled upon desserts, fair and equal portions had to be assigned or the howls were strong. One woman in help when I was very young couldn't stand the pressure of seven watchful child-faces while she fixed our whipped cream desserts; she insisted that Mother or Lizzie take on this awful responsibility. We used to laugh at her timid ways and crumbled self-confidence, but some years later she hanged herself from the basement beam of her home in town. When I heard of the suicide I remembered our dessert clamor and felt saddened by the greed of the world, which so dreadfully impinged upon her need to be loved for herself alone—not just for the cream she dispensed.

Grandfather had such a dislike of cheese he and his children scorned those who could stomach such smelly, sour stuff. But since Mother's people were great cheese fanciers, we acquired a keen taste for it and teased Uncle Jack for turning up his nose. After curds had formed in the sour milk, Mother lumped them together in two cheesecloth bags and suspended them from the warming-oven door handles of the stove, for the whey to drip into dishpans below. These white, breastlike bags would hang overnight, and every now and then in the evening, somebody would knead them a little, massaging them. Next day's yield of cottage cheese would disappear in a few days, for we relished the delicacy precisely because it figured in the slight contention between the women of our household and the male, German side of it.

Ice cream, the very apotheosis of milk, tasted best on hot summer days, but unfortunately the milch cows were in their slack period then. Sometimes after a late spring calf, Molly or Dolly still produced sufficiently for us to make ice cream for my birthday, June 27, or even for the Fourth of July. No child minded the labor of turning the freezer handle but fought over the privilege, in order to lick the dasher, afterwards. A block of ice was purchased in town and chipped into pieces, packed into the small wooden barrel, around the metal custard container, then salted to lower the temperature. Any commercial flavor tasted at confectioners' we tried to match at home with our own strawberries, black and red raspberries, cherries, and concocted some flavors nobody'd heard of: such as mulberry and Juneberry ice cream. According to a movie magazine, Ginger Rogers indulged a childhood dream by installing an ice-cream-soda fountain in her Hollywood home. We fancied a heavenly someday when we might devour really all the ice cream we craved, only to have it happen miraculously a snowy winter morning when an ice-cream truck got embedded in drifts near the country schoolhouse. The teacher, Miss Flock, dismissed us all so that we could help shovel and push—and for reward the driver gave us a container of strawberry ice cream. We sat down to it immediately, for Miss Flock didn't believe in postponing pleasure, and with the stove fired up

to keep off the chill consumed it all—most of us getting awfully sick. One more trapping of a dream which we didn't have
to carry into adulthood.

Daily, we downed our glasses of milk seriously, feeding our
bones, and wiped the white mustaches from our lips. Milk
would make our teeth strong, give us stamina. Proof of this
magic diet was the way we all grew, inches taller than the
previous generation. What had been good for us as babies
(breast-fed, every one of us) kept on being good: glasses of
milk late at night, cold from the refrigerator, and first thing
after school, with graham crackers or bread and jam. Following
a sick period of vomiting, our recovery nourishment was
always boiled milk with floes of toast. One year, a return-to-
visit hired girl, now married and with a new baby, opened
her blouse and lifted out her heavy breast to let the infant
suck right there in the living room—showing us all what she
now had but which in her slim girlhood we hadn't, somehow,
given her credit for.

Saturday mornings during the school year, we could sleep as
late as we wished, and when we arose fixed our own breakfasts
from the box cereals left on a corner of the oilcloth and dipped
into the bowl of fresh grapefruit sections, which Lizzie had prepared the night before. Our late sleeping was tolerated for the
good reason of our health, but we still caught the farm shame
of such malingering. Chores and jobs and the whirl of the day
had long since passed us by, and we'd never catch up. But one
thing I knew: no matter the hour, my first task was to churn.
Lizzie would bring out the bright blue painted metal box with
gold lettering on the side and place it into the silvered steel
frame. Little wooden doors fitted neatly on top, with a center
hole for the shaft. She'd pour in the can of sour cream, strong
and slightly nauseating in odor—at that hour of the morning.
Often in summer the cream would be too warm, and it lingered
in liquid state forever before finally collapsing into butter. In the
most fortunate churnings, I always had at least half an hour of
work ahead of me, turning the crank, first sitting down and
spinning the wheel indifferently, as if it weren't my enemy;

then standing up earnestly and hunching over the churn, like pumping a bicycle to make a tough hill. But going too fast accomplished nothing, as Lizzie would remind me—speed didn't matter—it was persistence that counted. Butter would only form in its own mysterious good time, no matter what I did.

The wooden paddle wheel turned *slop-slop* in easy liquid the first ten or fifteen minutes. Every now and then we'd have a look—a sour milk reeking womb—and with a long spatula Lizzie would strip down the sides and scrape off the wooden doors, though we both knew that once I started up again the liquid would splatter all over the inside, just as before. I tried to set goals—that by the time I counted two hundred turns of the wheel I'd have butter, or four hundred, or one thousand. Meanwhile, my scot-free younger cousin was curled up close to the radio, tuned to "Let's Pretend," listening to the sweet, somewhat sinister voice of that enticing lady who got the story started, and her friends, those falsetto fairies.

Mesmerized by my rhythm at the handle, sometimes I'd forget time entirely, and Lizzie would come into the kitchen from outdoors and say, "What? You're still at it? Let's have a look." If the cream had gotten too warm, all of it was put back into the refrigerator and I'd start over again later. When the cranking became harder, I knew the paddle was spinning in whipped cream—that I must now strenuously press forward to beat the reluctant liquid, master it, whack the living daylights out of it, shatter the heavy mountainous piles that suddenly welled up, almost to the top, struggling to be stronger than me —until suddenly it all gave up and splattered into butter-islands, bits and hunks here and there. Done in, vanquished. The mopping-up operation was accomplished quickly: a fast recollecting inside there, as all the butter hastily found remnants of itself and chunked together into impossible-to-break-up mounds. "Enough! Enough!" Lizzie cried, hearing the butter-milk slosh and the butter thump. "You're through! Through!" And the world at the creation must have come together in this manner too, the elements all in flux and God the mixer.

Lizzie would pile the land mass of pale yellow butter into an ocean-blue crock and go to work with a wooden butter paddle, forming and reforming this malleable, newly created globe. Watery liquid was squeezed and slapped out of it, the butter salted and separated into small planets for placement into bowls, to be stored in the Frigidaire. None of us children cared for buttermilk, but Mother and Aunt Lizzie didn't mind and saved this delicious drink as a treat for themselves.

The sickly, pale natural color of butter would change in spring when the Holsteins found new, succulent grass. They gave thanks to the season's advent in their deep-gold butter. We were never far from the pleasure a plant took in growing, an animal in living. At night I'd stare heavenward at the curds of stars called the Milky Way. In a galaxy of such infinite milkiness, we were alive and attentive here at the nourishing breast of the world.

6. The Eighty

No one had ever lived there. The eighty acres Grandfather purchased half a mile west of the farm after he'd settled the homestead was the wild land itself, the indifferent earth, which could get along without us. Each spring dark green stripes of new grass marked the old wagon trail to the county seat, in use before surveying straightened out neat mile-square sections. But actual ruts could never be found, for only the land held memory of those days; manure from horses and oxen drawing wagons had seeped into the ruts and stayed there, enriching the soil for decades.

Because one fourth of the Eighty was low and wet, Grandfather laid tiles for drainage, a co-operative venture with the neighbors, their tiles connecting with ours. The runoff gathered in a tributary of the Little Sioux River, which drained into the Missouri at Sioux City, into the Mississippi at St. Louis, and finally into the Gulf of Mexico. The throaty gurgle of the tiles only a few feet below the surface was the music of journey, of the long voyage to the sea; I felt opened by it, freed. All seven of us children in this inland fastness would make such an outward trip too; we had different notions of our destinies, but each of us was heading out. We were being nourished here for such travelings, storing up all that might be needed, and, like the water in the tiles, we'd never be back.

We hungered to know more about the earth as it had been before pioneering Grandfather arrived, and Uncle Jack showed us the tough-bladed buffalo grass growing along a western fence, virgin prairie, the fence row having preserved the sod from the plow. Since the neighbors' cattle, leaning through the barbed wire, had clipped the blades short, we never witnessed the grass in full six-foot height the way it had been. Yet, the Eighty with its prairie wild flowers and birds, open skies, was our wilderness.

Summers, I'd ride a bicycle out each day to check my trap line. Ground-squirrel tails yielded five cents each when brought to the county courthouse for bounty. The simple trap, a spring pincers with a paddle trip, was placed directly on top of the hard, plain hole. When the squirrel popped out head first he hit the paddle and sprang the trap. To induce the squirrel's appearance, we sometimes poured buckets of water down exit holes nearby we assumed were back doors, but it usually took more water than we could haul to the spot. Pocket-gopher traps were more complicated: lean and long like the vertebrae of a gopher, neatly fitting into the tubular entrance after one removed the mound of finely pulverized earth. Then, with primitive cunning, one covered the hole the way it had been, marking the faint circle of the hole itself, just as the gopher drew it (with his paw? his breath?). The chopped-off front legs of a gopher brought ten cents.

Badgers inhabited the steepest hillside of the Eighty, devouring corn and chewing alfalfa roots—an enemy of farmers and therefore of our county government, but the wonder of such exotic creatures living their wild days in close proximity to ours kept us from destroying them for bounty. Foxes, even more romantic, leapt out of Red Riding Hood's terror to lope down the back fence rows, tails afloat. They didn't rob our chicken roosts because pheasants were plentiful quarry. But one autumn Uncle Jack shot a fox from his corn picker. I lifted its rear canine legs (scarcely able to!), had my picture taken as though I'd slain it, and sometimes in dimming memory I think I did. This silky, wild-smelling creature, more beautiful than a pet dog, was awfully heavy dead. I felt the wrongness of such a killing, a distant, uneasy threat of violence to *me,* somewhere in a final reckoning. But I came to this consciousness slowly, only after leaving the land—for every farmer must be a killer.

The Eighty took the season's changes most purely, since man had asserted himself over Nature only a little in raising crops for his purposes, not hers. No trees flourished to provide shade on a hot haying day, for there'd never been trees on the prairie; in winter nothing stopped the raw blast of the northwest wind. In the slough wild strawberries grew low enough to escape the sickle bar of the mower—small buds of strawberry essence, a far cry from the Fairfax berries the older boys set out in an orchard at home, harvested by exploited younger brothers and sisters who toiled up and down the rows with wooden quart boxes—to fill crates which would be sold at the grocery store for a few dollars. Of which we got nothing. Everybody had chores and money coming into the family supposedly benefited all, but we underlings didn't like it, suspected graft. The berries were massive, juicy, but lacking the strong flavor of those wild ones in the Eighty, which couldn't be marketed or even picked in quantities; so fragile they squashed immediately and had to be eaten on the spot. Cultivation—husbandry—was the beginning of fakery and manipulation.

Compared to Grandpa's homestead, the Eighty was not especially rich land; weeds knew and thrived there. Mornings in early summer Uncle Jack deployed us, each kid armed with a hoe, assigned to hack thistles from the corn rows, chopping out the roots if possible. In July we marched again through the afflicted cornfields, this time to unwrap morning-glory vines strangling the plants. Even the slough, which wound around the hillocks, making a massive Y design in the valley, was ravaged by ironweeds, burdock, marijuana, milkweed, and ragweed. We'd yank them out too unless a red-winged blackbird had already built a nest in a weed crotch, or a dick-cissel—Uncle Jack's favorite, for it's jaunty whistling song and dapper spot of black on yellow breast.

Horses were no longer harnessed to the mower for cutting slough grass. Instead, I sat in the big-bottomed seat of the mower, which was drawn by Jack's tractor, and operated the levers controlling the sickle bar. Approaching rough turf that might clog the shifting blades, or when turning (so that cut grass wouldn't bunch up), I'd lift the many-bladed, heavy bar, hanging with all my weight on the upright lever, inhaling exhaust fumes and the sweet aroma of new-cut grass. Jack carefully steered around known birds' nests in the tall weeds; afterwards, islands of vegetation lay here and there in the savanna, the rightful claim of birds. Jack would signal when to lift the shuttling blades, or I'd do it myself fast, if a meadowlark flew out of its nest at the last possible moment, or a hen-pheasant. Since no pheasant returned to an exposed nest, we'd stop and gather the eggs carefully in Jack's blue bandanna, later tuck them under stupid setting hens, who'd raise the tawny, speckled chicks as their own. When a nice gawky size we'd have them for Sunday dinner instead of spring chicken, gloating over the fact that we hadn't had to shoot them, and that they'd never even known they were pheasants.

After the bluegrass was cut the mucky soil lay exposed but seldom dried; save for the grass, a creek might have formed. In the center it was usually too wet to drive machinery through, and that waving grass would stand like a strip of swamp, presided over by chevroned red-winged blackbirds. With the luck of good weather after mowing, the grass properly sun-cured, I'd be on the windrower: a huge, rickety rake, the half-circle tines aimed at the ground. I'd sweep the hay into fluffy windrows which the hay loader later picked up. Jack and I would scoot up and down the slough, finishing the job in half a day, sometimes in just a few hours.

The hay loader, a conveyor-belt contraption powered by gears from the moving wheels, was best pulled by a team of slow horses. We hitched up our only two nags and gave them a summer outing. The hay loader was attached to the rear of the hayrack. Prongs whisked the hay from the ground to a canvas belt, which carried it up into the wagon, where I waited with a pitchfork. I'd spread the stuff around, steadily building the load, myself standing higher and higher until at last, with the hay clogging together, I shouted *stop! stop!* to the horse driver. Then I rested in the stickery, sweet-smelling hay, sank down exhausted, straw hat released but still shading my brow, liking the rank odor of sweat, straw, and leather hatband; rocking and lolling as we wound our way home, drawn by those ancient horses, Sam and Babe, each lurch easing the load into a feeling for itself. Cars might pass below, hurrying ahead of their own dust, but I was high above such civilized nuisances, lord of the countryside, on an eye level with meadowlarks on telephone wires—in a nest myself, luxuriant.

The hired man and older boys were waiting in the haymow. The previous hayrack had been rolled empty out of the barn, one man guiding the tongue on the wild ride down the earthen ramp. Now the horses must be made to quicken their pace and gain momentum in order to haul the load up into the haymow. We'd slap the reins on their gaunt backs, calling courage, and up we'd go. After unhitching the horses and leading them away, the great, tined hayfork that hung from the track on the ridgepole was guided into place overhead, poised above the load. The metal fork, polished silver from having plunged into so much hay, dropped from the ceiling to the hayrack with fierce strength. A man would set it deep, like a fork into a plate of sauerkraut. And if the set was good, when the horses reared back, pulling a rope to lift it, nearly a quarter of the load would rise up, up, to the ceiling, hit a traverse and swing along until it reached the intended mow, where it would be tripped and hay would cascade down. At first this wilted grass stacked in the haymow looked captured, forlorn, lost from its land of the Eighty, but in a week it all belonged to the barn; it had become hay.

Some years the corn borers weakened stalks; the heavy ears fell too low to be snatched by the corn picker in October. These kernels would sprout like weeds in next year's oats field or spoil the soybeans. To prevent this, we picked up ears by hand, tossing them into a truck box or tractor-hauled wagon, gathering an entire load on a few acres. School was well underway by then and we'd only gather lost ears of corn on Saturdays, though sometimes Mother and Aunt Lizzie would go to the fields for the fun of it on a weekday, a change from housekeeping, work more serious and significant because closer connected to money income. (But they believed such tasks were not ordinarily proper for today's self-respecting farm ladies, though their pioneer mothers helped the men in barn and field.)

November Saturdays of picking up corn: back once again in the closest nest of all. After weekday forays in alien town classrooms, thoughts on future city careers and distant commercial successes, I'd expended vital stores that need replenishing. The marshaling of the family work force pleased Jack, too, and his good spirits bolstered ours. In a similar way, our hog and cattle feeding chores after school were a kind of fertilizing relief. Off with the tight city shoes, creased trousers, ironed shirt; into shoulder-hooked overalls and cowhide work shoes— walk toward the barns, one's body feeling loose and strong, kicking away the cramp school desk. The silage I hauled to the cattle still smelled of September. Pitching hay down from the dusty mow, sneezing, feeling the chaff and pollen itchy on arms and neck, it was summer all over again.

When human gleaning of the Eighty ended, the entire acreage became a grange for our field herd of black Angus. They'd find corn we hadn't, eat the rich slough grass, and munch the resprouting oats field before winter killed everything. We seldom fed more than fifty or sixty cattle, yet for the cattle drive to the Eighty all available children stood guard at each possible astray route along the way, waved hands and cried, "whoooosha! whoooosha!" hustling them along at a moderately excited pace. Out the farm road gate, filling up the thoroughfare, headed west. At the crossroads a quarter mile away, two boy sentinels stopped cars, spread arms wide to the loose animals. The older cattle knew where they were going and liked the idea, eager to be rid of our regular-hour bushel-basket feeding; glad to quit the familiar pastures clipped to the roots, tired of waiting for the tufts to hurry up and grow—knowing what loop in the fence allowed them to reach heads through for a morsel of forbidden, long ditch grass, or where a cowplop made the dark green blades delicious. After they'd all arrived safely, we shut the gate on their unfenced realm: eighty acres to move around on, the only shelter the leeward side of a strawstack created during July threshing and not very big; in a month they'd have demolished all of it. Here they were allowed to go primitive; after a time in the Eighty they were noticeably wilder-eyed, skittered when an automobile approached, or lumbered off like bison if a man came too near. They were on the range of their ancestors and reverting fast.

Winter was upon us when it was time to drive the herd home. The last freedoms of movement upon the soil were over for everybody, and we'd soon be struggling through drifts up to our ears. By late November the cattle looked fatter, their coats thickened to a rich, furry black, like the Alaska seal coats my two maiden aunts wore. The black, lowing herd, staccato hoofs on frozen ground, would surprisingly fill the farmyard from barns to garden fence. We were all cowboys then.

But one winter Uncle Jack left the herd in the Eighty too long. A terrible blizzard swept across the plains from the Rocky Mountains. We heard weather reports on the 6 A.M. news, and family counsel decided we shouldn't go to school, the roads would be closed. All of us were needed to rescue the cattle stranded in the Eighty. We bundled up in double overalls, one pulled over the other, buckle overshoes, blanket-lined jackets, and helmets with ear flaps, a muffler around mouth and nose. Only our eyes peeped out from below the leather helmet rim; if necessary, we could push up the wool cloth and still see through the interstices of weave. The women were alarmed for our safety, but the crisis of the herd in the Eighty

was overriding. As we turned out the road gate in the Model
A Ford, beyond the barrier of evergreens we could scarcely
navigate the drifts. Great stream-lined banks, dunelike shapes,
were alive and growing across the ditch, spuming snow. We
gunned the motor to keep momentum, and when we reached
the Eighty, found the murmuring cattle in a clump by the
closed gate, reproachful over our late arrival. In their bones
they'd felt the storm coming days before and wondered, no
doubt, why *we* hadn't—life knowledge they possessed but which
we'd deliberately moved away from in order to achieve a
consciousness of ourselves, in order to use Nature for our
purposes.

The cattle huddled with backs to the strong northwest wind,
heads away from the sharp snow, which came streaking on a
parallel with the ground. They were cattle-snowmen, every
detail etched in frost, lashes hoary, whiskers and nostrils ice-
encased; even with rumps to the storm, by morning they'd have
suffocated from ice filling their noses. After we shoveled open
the gate, they needed no encouragement; their leaders knew the
direction of our warm barns and turned east without paying
attention to me standing guard, not even a wrong lunge in fun.

Uncle Jack spotted the gangly, small calf, born perhaps
two weeks previously, huddled close to its mother, the snow
binding them together, encasing them in a womb of winter.
Jack swooped the calf up in his arms, collapsing the stalky legs
as you would a folding chair, and the frightened, half-dead
baby sat there like those pictures in Sunday school books of the
lamb in Jesus' arms. "Here, Ruthie, this one's for you," said
Jack to my sister, who of course insisted on coming along
with us boys on this adventure. She climbed into the back seat
of the auto, the calf on her lap big as a dog, blue eyes blinking,
and I marveled how the docile baby accepted any female love.
The iced snow around his muzzle began to melt and he trembled
all over. Ruth hugged him as she rubbed his coiled black hair.
Though born here in the wilderness, he now knew domesticity
was his true circumstance; he needed us in order to live. But
I didn't carry it further: that his eventual death in the slaughter-

house in Sioux City was to be his inevitable fate, so that we could make our living.

There wasn't a day in summer one didn't kill what was happily alive, out of the farmer's rationale of necessity: weeds choking vegetables, rats eating corn; potato bugs not snatched by the yearly visit of a flock of grosbeaks we'd capture by hand and drop into kerosene cans; I'd swing chickens around by the legs until they were dizzy, then head on the stained chopping block and down with the hatchet—served up smelling good a couple hours later at our dining table. Only when I heard the Colt .45 pistol shot and knew Jack was shooting a pig between the eyes for February butchering did the horror of killing come unavoidably forward.

But even farmers weren't on top. Nature could subdue us at any moment with storms, crop blights, drought, and so our conscience over slaughtered animals, plants, insects, and birds were salved, our guilt expiated by Nature's random authority over us. Our reason hadn't yet killed our faith and we took the signs of God humbly. The birds, animals, even plants knew something we didn't—or had forgotten, or couldn't quite grasp. My eleven-year-old cousin Lloyd, playing beside me with the Erector set one day, building bridges, became sick in the night and was dead next day of appendicitis. We bore the shocks and sorrows of our lives as other creatures did theirs, all afflicted with natural and unnatural enemies.

As the calf in the car got warmer he became wriggly, and Ruth finally had to sit on top to hold him on the seat. The hired man, looking through the window, asked her with a smile, "Did you *kill* that calf?"

How we all laughed!

During the Dust Bowl years of drought in the mid-Thirties, our homestead wells sank lower and lower, though never actually gave out. To preserve what underground veins still ran, so as not to draw too heavily for livestock watering, Uncle Jack decided to dig a well in the slough of the Eighty, the wettest, most certain resource of water on our land.

There were serious adult discussions over whether to employ the dowser who served our region. "Ridiculous superstition," according to Mother, and Aunt Lizzie wasn't at all sure we weren't trafficking with the Devil—it hardly seemed the sort of faith our church minister would approve of. But Jack recalled Grandpa had used a dowser for all his wells, and what had been good enough then was certainly all right now. In fact, since you didn't dig a well every day—none had been sunk on our farm for a quarter of a century—here was something unusual, educational, for the children to witness. Might never have another chance.

He put in a call for the dowser, and one day an albino appeared at our gate, eyes reddish as a rabbit's, eyelashes white, head licelike. We watched from a respectful, quiet distance as the man set out alone through the surf of bluegrass on his search for water, which all of us knew lay everywhere just a few feet below the surface (though these years even the tiles no longer gurgled). With his pronged apple witching wand ahead of him like a blind man's cane, he walked as if mesmerized through the slough. Suddenly the apple bough bucked, plunged, seemed about to fly out of his hand, eager to bury itself into some deep fountain the apple sap longed for. Here the spot was marked with a creosoted post—the center of the Y where the branches of tile met. The well-diggers later would have to take care not to break into the tile system.

Uncle Jack didn't want the albino fun to be over so quickly. Where were other good spots—for future wells? He sent the hoary dowser off across the right arm of the Y in a northwesterly direction. Soon the bough quivered, shook, danced in the air and sank to the earth. But when the digging equipment arrived the following week, the first place was chosen and water was found six feet down. In later, wet years, I peered under the plank roof of the well at the mirrored black water just three or four feet below and had the feeling our Eighty was really an enormous island. If I jumped up and down hard, like on a raft, I might set the whole surface rocking.

A windmill was erected, low over the well since nothing obstructed the breeze. The paddle fan pumped water into a large storage tank elevated on posts, high enough for a water wagon to pull under, fill up. Day after day tankloads were hauled to our thirsty cattle and hogs, the metal cold, sweaty, oceans of liquid sloshing inside. We wondered how the water of the Eighty tasted, for minerals flavored each farm family's wells somewhat differently. We thought our well water near the house couldn't be matched, and in helping neighbors during harvest, tasted drinking water we wondered they could bear. But only Uncle Jack could safely drink untested water because during World War I, when he was in the Army, he'd received typhoid shots, would be immune to any germs; we didn't question this.

Now with the new well, our black Angus cattle pastured in the Eighty after corn picking had a steady water supply. The storage tank, lowered to the ground, made a trough for them. In the worst of the drought years, which were seven in number, just as Joseph endured in Egypt, the well remained full and many neighbors drew off a tankful now and then. They came from far away in rattling water carts, and still the underground river flowed. Even the town fathers (two miles away) heard of our well and marked it as an emergency source in case of fire.

The end of the dry period came like a typhoon one late-summer day. Tornado and hail warnings were broadcast from all radio stations nearby, and dark, greenish-tinged clouds gathered in the west. A torrential rain, three inches in less than forty-five minutes, fell upon us. The homemade earthen dam in the farmyard was swept away, the garden washed out, birds' nests lay on the ground. We'd never seen such water. During the great 1930's floods of the Ohio River Valley, hearing of marooned families in Cairo, Illinois, floating houses, abandoned cars, and drowned children, I'd been reassured by the adults that our farm was on safe high ground. And yet on this day Uncle Jack reported that the entire Eighty was flooded, the crops ruined. Cornstalks stuck in the fence at the lowest end had built a dam of debris which backed up a whole lake of water. *This* was something we must surely see! He was more excited about the curiosity of the event than chagrined over his spoiled hay lands and demolished grain fields; or rather, since a farmer could do nothing about what Nature decided to mete out to him, one might as well, philosophically, take what pleasures could be found. We clambered into the car and drove down the squishy road to the Eighty to see our sudden lake.

Now the windmill was a gaunt diver's tower over a great lagoon, and the eight-foot metal cattle trough was afloat. "Look —look, a boat!" We *had* to get in, have a boat ride while we could. The older boys rolled up pants' legs and splashed into the chocolate-colored water, captured the tank. We leapt into the make-believe skiff and set off, poling our way with long sticks we found floating. Sometimes we became stranded on a sandbar-like bottom, had to step out into the water to push off, but at last we were floating in the middle of the slough, Jack smiling and relishing our fun—from the cornfield shore.

At the far end of the Eighty, Barney the hired man was already pulling away stalks and trying to salvage the fence, but he only succeeded in ripping U-nails from the fence posts; and suddenly, as if the plug had been let out of a giant tub, the whole lake began to move—the fence dam collapsed. We were adrift, carried by the momentum of water—to the river and the sea! At first our progress was slow as a riverboat's, then we moved faster and faster, behind us a muddy wake that feathered out and disappeared.

I crawled to the helm of the cattle trough, to be in the front spot for this magnificent journey, moving from land to ocean, Uncle Jack growing smaller in the distance. How we shouted our exultation over this release from our lives; outgoing—away from childhood, away from the Eighty, into the tributaries of the world and the strange life that lay ahead in time, beyond our horizons, to which we all aspired.

Then I heard Uncle Jack's hoarse voice calling us back—or warning us. Was he begging us not to leave him? Not to so outdistance our too young lives that we couldn't go back if we wanted to, if we had to? No, for just a moment I wondered, How odd for him to be worried, since he'd never doubted our abilities to get on in the world. He was always preparing us, equipping us to make our way. He himself hadn't wanted to be a farmer, although he'd grown up on the land—had slipped away for just a while when in the Army, but marriage and Grandfather had drawn him back and held him, a fate he knew wouldn't happen to us. Yet now as we cascaded along down the wide river and away from the Eighty, why was he yelling and waving so frantically?

I looked up and saw what he meant: over the entire bruise-blue eastern sky was a huge rainbow wishbone, the brilliant-hued misty end of it lay ahead of us just over the hill, or just beyond the hill beyond that, so close you could see the neighbors' black grove behind it. Never had the pot of gold been so near. We sailed on in our metal tub until we ran aground in a pasture on the other side of our fence line; while trying to get ourselves afloat again, the water receded rapidly. We pushed and struggled with the cattle trough but couldn't find water deep enough for buoyancy. And by the time we looked up again the rainbow was gone.

7. Barney

Barney, the hired man, found his way to our homestead from his native Friesland, in Holland, through a brother already established as a farm hand in the neighborhood. Jack needed help after Father died, and the idea of providing a job for an immigrant appealed to his give-a-man-a-chance Americanism. Having served in the Army and now a prominent member of the American Legion, Jack felt particularly qualified to tutor a greenhorn in how to become part of this great land. Furthermore, with men out of work and the Hoover government unable to cope with the nation's problems, helping a wide-eyed newcomer reach citizenship bolstered our faith in America, land of opportunity. Barney wouldn't expect much in wages, either—being grateful for his fortunate placement with us. It was a mild form of indenture, at least until he received his first papers and no longer needed a sponsor.

Barney learned most of his English from us children, though we didn't realize we were teaching him. He sat listening during meals at the big kitchen table, extended with three or four leaves in order to accommodate seven children, four adults, plus one step-cousin who boarded with us during the school year for twenty dollars a month. Self-effacing, trying to oblige any requests made of him, Barney bided his time and did his work. He grinned a little too much, always did what Jack asked of him, and never laid a hand on us no matter how wicked we were or how much we teased him. His eye on us commanded no force of censure; he was totally unarmed by his position. We took his second-class status in our household as matter-of-factly as Southerners might regard Negro servants. No matter how badly we were jumped on or humiliated by a sibling or scolded by a parent, Barney was handy to feel superior to, for he was a foreigner and knew it. He could scarcely talk at all, and then in a thick-tongued way which made us laugh. He soon discarded the high-crown European hat, and in overalls almost passed for a native, but he couldn't afford to get rid of the oddly cut, tight suit with the baggy pants, and for best still wore his pointy Dutch shoes of light tan leather. We could always come to a sense of peace about ourselves, knowing that at least we were better off than Barney!

He was blue-eyed and fair-skinned, with reddish blond hair; stockily built, not tall like the men of our family but thickly muscled and with a large chest and the stamina of a Percheron horse. He was friendly toward us but never actually touched any of the master's children, nor did we come close to his person—though near enough to note he had a faint body odor that didn't resemble anyone else's. It probably derived from his nasty habit of chewing plugs of tobacco, which he may have taken up since smoking was forbidden in our Lutheran household. His sweet-smelling packet of Red Chief chewing tobacco bulged in his upper shirt pocket like one breast. The brown cud in his mouth became visible only when he let fly at a weed—the expectoration such a surprisingly willful act we found it strange. He clearly wasn't choking on phlegm but doing it for fun. Adults, when asked about a man's craving for chewing tobacco, laughingly shook their heads, for such habits were the sort of thing one might expect from someone just over from the old country.

Forever curious about the language of communication between creatures, we tried to figure out just what the livestock

said to one another (the pigeons talked about the weather—
it's going to be coooooool, it's going to be coooooool), and
although Barney's Dutch was gibberish to us, he was understood
by the animals. His mutterings to the milch cows made them
let down their milk, and his singsong baaaing, *s'calvic, s'calvic,
calvic,* to the calves in the evening, when he carried skimmed
milk to them, was almost as good as a mother's voice, from
the reaction it caused.

Uncle Jack always chose machinery to do farmwork, when he
could, for he was allied with the future, but Barney stuck to
Sam and Babe, hitching up our only pair of horses as if
married to them, going off to the fields in their company. Europe
and the past signified just such couplings of man and beast,
whereas America and the progress of technology meant cold
and impersonal connections between man and motor—a clean,
hard, unambiguous relationship, intellect mastering inanimate
machinery. Of such an advance Barney would be incapable.
He couldn't understand the simplest automobile engine and
electricity was sorcery. Jack tried to indoctrinate him in ordinary
mechanics, but understandably, considering Barney's stodgy
past and present language difficulties, only a small amount got
through. Barney was allowed to continue with what he knew
best: his hand on the flank of rusty-gold, sway-backed Sam or
black-coated Babe was the perfect touch for their domestic
obedience.

Because Barney was an *Ausländer,* we knew he wouldn't be
accustomed to modern devices such as indoor toilets and therefore thought nothing wrong with the arrangement whereby he
was to accommodate himself in the outhouse, even in below-
zero weather. Nor were Europeans famous for bodily cleanliness,
and since Barney had surely never used a bathtub in Holland,
he didn't step into ours on Saturday nights but instead took
sponge baths in a dishpan of hot water, carrying teakettles upstairs to his room over the kitchen.

That room was the only chamber in the house forbidden to
our curious explorations. When he was up there moving about
on the creaking floor boards, we could scarcely stand the mystery

of the place. A crooked, steep little stair led to this under-the-roof bedroom, the top floor of the old farmhouse built in the 1880's, before the new house had been attached at the turn of the century. The room was plaster-finished and insulated, but the only heat flowed through the hot-air register directly over the kitchen range. Barney would stand on top of the vent to dress on bitterly cold winter mornings, when ice had frozen in his water pitcher. Since Barney wasn't a full participant in our family life, his very separation—which our attitudes forced upon him—meant his private life was a tantalizing unknown, and to plumb the depths of his difference became our obsession.

We waited our chance: a Wednesday afternoon when the women were off to Ladies' Aid and the men in the fields. The staircase door always stuck from the difference in temperature between the hot kitchen and chill upstairs. The sight of the steps thrilled us—wickedly steep and twisting sharply at the top, where flour barrels had once stood. We remembered the story of the one occasion when everybody had had the laugh on Grandpa. He accidentally tipped over a blue tin flour barrel, spilling flour all over him, and as he stumbled backwards down the steps and into the kitchen—a veritable snowman—how his children laughed! And he could do nothing about it, since he deserved it. Now the barrels were gone and the room seemed pathetically bare. Barney had made his bed neatly, even though he expected nobody to see it but himself. Our glances fell upon the painted plaster plaque of the Virgin and Child hung on the chimney. The power of the Catholic religion permeated the atmosphere: *this* was his secret self, never allowed downstairs among us Lutherans. We felt the Middle Ages leaping at us and wondered if Barney knelt before the Virgin and worshiped her, for one of the worst things about Catholics was their adoration of saints (not God or Jesus) and other peripheral heavenly beings, and the way they prayed to statues. On his oak commode stood a little black wooden cross with a maggoty Jesus hanging on it. Perhaps in the drawer lay a slithery strand of rosary beads, but the idea was too terrifying to pursue and we didn't investigate, for like a snake it might jump out at us.

We peeped at Barney's clothes in the beaverboard closet; not many of them, and we'd seen them all on his back. We turned to hunt more items, probe other secrets, but aside from the prevailing Roman Catholicity of the place, there was nothing much in the dreary room, with its small, sleepy windows under the eaves; a single iron prison bed with sagging springs, a spindle-back chair. No photograph of a funny-looking foreign family on his chest of drawers, no fond eyes of sweetheart or mother to look at him naked when he took off his clothes to go to bed. No Dutch language book for us to peruse and titillate ourselves over Barney's Continental difference—not even a Bible (but then, we'd been told Catholics seldom read the Bible, for if they ever did they'd turn into Lutherans).

We left Barney's bedroom with a new knowledge: that whatever he truly was, in unguarded openness, only people elsewhere saw it, when he left the farm Saturday nights. The notion of celebrating the Sabbath eve, with the attendant sins of drink and sex, struck us as a very Catholic attitude. In our Protestant hearts we knew God wasn't fooled by this all too human attempt to get away with a little pleasure, knowing Sunday confessional and mass would bring forgiveness. Such a Lord was not *our* Lord, who knew our inmost sins even before they were committed, who never let us get away with anything. Saturday night carousing was also lower-class, a desire for orgy that moved mostly in people who had little control over their lives and only existed day by day. We had more at stake, plans for the future, and took smug satisfaction in quiet Saturday evenings, only distantly attuned to the country's revelry by listening to "The Hit Parade" on the radio. We bathed under the red eye of the electric reflector-heater and the kerosene portable stove, then climbed into bed, since we had to be up early next day for church.

Barney finished Saturday night chores quickly, shaved, bathed, and backed out his Model T jalopy from the machine shed, where he kept it, since the garage had been built for only one car. He'd not return until very, very late, and we'd note his pasty look and the bags under his eyes next morning at breakfast. Of course, Jack, being his sponsor, had to keep abreast of Barney's midnight doings and worried aloud; once Barney left the wholesome atmosphere of our farm, he risked getting into trouble. Should something irregular happen, he could be deported—just like that! Back to Holland—or worse, Barney might become the Man Without a Country.

Time and again, Jack warned Barney about his cronies: "Those loafers you hang out with are only interested in spending your hard-earned money. Don't kid yourself." Barney bought them drinks to make them think him a good fellow, and they took advantage of his naïve eagerness. He always lost at cards and was seen in the company of questionable women from out of town, who spent every cent in his pockets. Neighbors reported to Jack any little news on Barney, for he was like a big muscular child who had to be let out now and then but who wasn't to be trusted with his own life. Barney, instead of resenting the paternalism, regarded Jack as his American father, though they were only a decade apart in years. Next-morning regrets always consumed him, but resolutions to mend his ways went no further than did his belief he'd actually follow the priest's admonition, "Go and sin no more."

"I don't care what he does with his cash—or his spare time," Jack would say to an informing neighbor, gossiping about Barney's latest escapade, "but I'd sure as hell hate to see him miss out on citizenship."

"If only they'd leave him alone until he's had a chance to know what's what," Lizzie would say.

"No, they want to use him while they can," said Jack.

Paying Barney's salary was a moment of embarrassment for Jack, for it defined the commercial arrangement and diminished the feeling that Barney was a sort of guest here on his way to becoming an American. He was remunerated as we children were (we got a dime for a bushel of dandelions dug out of the lawn, roots and all), as if one should be grateful anybody thought such labor could translate itself into hard coin. Barney worked from sunup milking to dusk calf-slopping and was expected to thank his employer for the privilege of being paid a dollar a day. The biggest favor we were doing was giving him the unique chance of becoming a citizen; for such an opportunity money was no equivalent. Like us children, Barney must learn to prepare himself for freedom and responsibility. We were expected to prove our mettle and remove all doubts from the Germanic, authoritarian-minded adults as to the worth of us, for childish looseness in deportment wasn't viewed as the natural bent of a human being in his development but rather as the deplorable tendency of the raw child toward shiftlessness, mischief, and wickedness. Our farm was a stopping point for Barney on the road to a better future, just as it was for us. With what faithful optimism we accepted the challenge of this movement in time! We never doubted but that the years ahead would be better and the anguish suffered now in striving for the highest grades and in long hours of farm work to earn money for college would be worth it. Our widowed mother's devotion of her after-forty life to the rearing of us and spending her small cash reserves on our schooling would eventually return to her the satisfaction of seeing us all launched in successful careers, esteemed by those who knew us in our new lives—and *that* would be reward enough! Likewise, Uncle Jack, who'd dreamt of becoming a mechanical engineer, would see his children get the opportunities denied him. The promise of our family was locked in securely so long as we children moved outward into our developing lives. The farm was gardenlike, a nurturing place, and the toil of wresting a living from the earth would be impetus to our ambitions, would enforce our determination to seek a livelihood by the exertion of one's brain rather than muscles. None of this had to be discussed. Farming was what a man did when he didn't have any particular skill or career, when he was ignorant, untrained. And so, when Barney arrived no one thought to ask if he'd actually come from a farm background—it was understood he did this work because farming was all a Dutch-speaking newcomer could manage. Years later I learned he was from a Netherlands town, and all he knew about animals, corn planting, haying, and milking, he'd picked up during his stay with us, learning the trade while acquiring the new language. His linguistic lag covered up his farm ignorance.

Barney's precise background was no history for him to acknowledge or go into, here in Iowa, for it was enough to admit he was from the old country, that place to be quickly forgotten if he wanted to get anywhere in the U.S.A. Barney received no mail from Holland—the stamp collectors among us would have leapt upon the letter if he had. We assumed that he and his brother (soon married and settled on a rented farm) were alone in life, without other family. Barney never seemed homesick and discussed nothing of his life "over there," nor were we encouraged to probe, since nostalgia might undo him. He'd have to make a clean cut, just as the pioneers of old had done. He studied the little citizenship book with facts about our country, the legislative system, how democracy worked; Mother and Lizzie would drill him on the right answers to questions in the text—when the kitchen was cleared of all auditors, so that easy-to-blush Barney wouldn't be embarrassed. The day he was to be examined and receive his first citizenship papers, Jack drove to Sioux City with him, along with Barney's brother. Barney passed beautifully and now had a firm foothold in America.

Meanwhile, the farmer's choicest crop, his own children, were coming along fine and we were soon old enough to help Jack run the farm. Those of us still in local schools undertook evening chores (he did the morning work himself); he milked only a couple of cows, cut down on his cattle feeding and fattened pigs instead, which were more profitable and easier to maintain. The older boys, home from college on vacations, were available for the heavy work of summer harvests. There was no longer need for a hired man, nor did Barney wish to linger, for he'd met through his brother a suitably Catholic Mary, and the banns were read in Church. She was not in her first youth, may have been all of thirty, and would therefore be grateful to Barney for having saved her from old-maidhood. Nor was she particularly sexy in appearance, but as a good woman should be,

subdued in dress, quiet in her ways; even her hair was trained
into severe little rolls and held by chains of bobby pins.

Barney's getting married! We tried not to think the idea
absurd, and certainly the sexual side was as unimaginable as
the bed life of one's parents; mostly, it seemed a good bargain
had been struck. No longer would *we* be responsible for looking
after him, fearing the quagmires of trouble he might stray into.
Mary would see to it that Barney's foolish, foreign, gullible
ways and his eagerness to win approval from the riffraff around
town wouldn't spoil his marvelous chances of making something
of himself. One sign of his improvement was the new job he
landed, working for the grain elevator in town—one step up,
out of the furrow. He still wore overalls around the giant bins
near the railroad tracks, but in the evening he'd walk home down
well-lighted streets, and Mary wouldn't have to contend with
manure tracked into the house on barnyard shoes. They were
town folk. At first they lived on the second floor of a big
yellow house on the central boulevard leading into town. We'd
pass by and stare at the windows, speculating about Barney's
new life, wondering what Mary really thought of him, once she
got to know him on the honeymoon. They giggled and blushed
happily whenever we happened to run into them. Mary was
soon pregnant.

With defense-plant jobs at high pay opening in the West,
Barney and Mary decided to move to Portland. Dressed in
town clothes, Barney's shirt and tie a sign demarking independence and equality, he came out to the farm to say good-by
to us. In his inarticulate, stumbling way, he tried to tell Lizzie
and Jack how grateful he felt for everything they'd done, that
we'd always seem like his true family. Or perhaps he said none
of this and I only interpreted his heartfelt farewell to embody
this message. His removal to the Pacific Northwest meant we'd
probably never lay eyes on him again, and this knowledge lent
an edge of poignancy to the parting. Yes, he'd write and tell
us how they were faring—or Mary would, since she knew the
language—and we'd be the first to know when the baby was
born!

Then, yearly photographs: first, a snapshot of an incredibly small development house on which he'd made a down payment, the monthly mortgage less than rent would have been. "Imagine, Barney owns a house!" We couldn't get over glorying in the wonders of the United States—for Barney to come so far in such a short time, with nothing but his hands and strong back at his disposal. Naturally, in Oregon nobody would know what a greenhorn he'd been when he first arrived. Barney's salary was a dizzying fifty dollars a week, which he turned over to Mary, who knew best how to manage, and they felt Jack would be pleased to hear some of the money was laid aside in government war bonds—helping out his adopted country.

Next year, a family portrait: baby looked square-faced and Dutch, Mary wider in the hips, big in the bosom; and Barney stood proudly next to her, teeth hanging out, hair almost gone on top, smiling to us back in Iowa as if to say: *See, see how I've done?* Each succeeding year in the Catholic way there was another infant, all girls, with white-yellow hair. Now the shrubs around their home had grown bigger, and the neighbors didn't seem quite so close. "By golly," Jack said, "I'd sure like to go out there and pay Barney a visit." But by this time sorrows were closing in on us. We knew Barney had gotten out with his hopes just in time; his forward-moving life couldn't draw strength from us now. He sent a sympathy card when he heard of Jack's son's death in an air collision in 1943, and he knew Mother had been operated on for cancer a few years earlier, was now partially paralyzed by a stroke. A pall had fallen over our household.

Barney's wages on the assembly line in Oregon rose higher and higher, for he was vigorous and able to put in many hours of overtime. Soon they moved into a commodious house. The oldest child enrolled in school and began to have a little history of her own. *This* girl liked to sing and play the piano, and *that* one was clever at drawing, hoped to become an artist. Barney and Mary produced seven children altogether—he succeeded in duplicating us, his first family. All the girls had bangs and long silky hair, just like our two used to have. Those children going off to their new brick city schools would think themselves Americans like anybody else, their father's accent the only reminder of days in the past outdistanced. Barney wouldn't recount the ignominy of a hired hand's life, if he felt any lingering shame, for his feelings had churned into warm gratitude toward us—that his transplantation from Holland to Iowa had given him the strength to be whatever it was he was to become in his life, here in the state of Oregon, where he was at last in the full stretch of his own freedom. It was out there he received his final citizenship papers and wrote proudly to Jack, telling how he stood before the flag.

8. Bringing in the Sheaves

The oats fields were tawny, dead-ripe; it was harvesttime. Before the slender straw stalks bent jointed knees, laid low in God's relentless will to have seeds mature, fall to the ground, and sprout again next spring, we farmers planned to intervene. Sundays in church our hymn-singing rose to God beyond the varnished rafters, and the minister's text was from Ruth: "So she gleaned in the field until even, and beat out that she had gleaned: and it was about an ephah of barley . . ." Ruth flourished in God's good favor not only because of her loyalty to Naomi but also for her husbandry, snatching from the ground what the harvesters had missed. And the young men of Boaz were touched, "and let fall also some of the handfuls of purpose for her, and leave them, that she may glean them . . ."

"Bringing *in* the sheaves . . . bringing *in* the sheaves!" In that hymn we offered our whole mortal selves to God's reaping, envisioning a harvest of harvests: the promised, glorious end to the burden of recurrent seasons on earth—the work of life over, pearly bliss eternal. Gentle hypocrites, who among us truly wanted the end to come just yet? Not in the middle of July!

Oats-cutting did not begin until all the growth in the plants had stopped and the seeds were fully sprung from the dry husks; otherwise, the moisture count would be too high and the price at market proportionately low. The risk was that the field might be flattened in a rainstorm or even by a strong wind; sometimes, if left too long, a grain field "lodged," the fragile stalks simply collapsed from fatigue and old age.

When Uncle Jack deemed the moment right, he hooked the tractor to the binder and pulled it creakingly out of storage in the machine shed. He lubricated every gear with his squirting oil can, a believer in generous anointment of his machinery: all that turned, metal against metal, got an oily bath, and the earth around the machine shed was darkly caked, like the early oiled roads before macadam.

The binder was a grass mower that had sprouted moth wings and contained a womb for the production of sheaves. Uncle Jack opened a grain field by driving the tractor into the waving oats, cutting a swath near the fence line, the binder behind him and out to the right, like a sidecar. The tractor, hub high in oats, was irremediably flattening a track that only the cattle, later on, would nibble and enjoy. On the next round we'd reverse the direction, and I'd be at the tractor wheel—he'd ride the binder. My tractor path was the clipped stretch of stubble next to the quadrangle of grain, which diminished in size with each round, until it was gone entirely.

Powered by link chains, the high, slatted spool of the binder, like the paddle wheel of a riverboat, gracefully turned with the moving wheels. The spool slats folded a six-foot sweep of oats plants toward the shuttling scissors that rode just above the ground. The snipped-off stalks were forced to lie down on a conveyor belt—sent into the middle of the machine like battalions of dead soldiers. There in the bundle-making compartment a sheaf would be formed, the oats embraced by twine, a cincture secured by a knot. The just-born bundle was emitted out the back, upon a claw-hand carrier. When a few sets of identical twins had accumulated, the operator tripped the carrier, dropping the bundles where the shockers could easily find them. Round and round the field I'd go, making a smaller and smaller square, careful to mow a full six-foot swath, but not so wide that I missed any oats. At last there'd be just an eyebrow standing, which I could mow down easily: the field was cut and bundles lay like fallen bodies everywhere.

In a week with fair weather, we'd cut all sixty or eighty acres of our oats and barley in various fields. The shockers, Barney, my older brothers and cousin, tried to keep up with us because a thunderstorm on stray bundles would knock some of the grain heads loose, or add to the wet count when the grain was sold at the Farmers' Elevator; or, if kept by us, increase the danger of spontaneous combustion in the granary. The fun of shocking was to create the little haycocks quickly and firmly. With the first bundle held by the twine waist in one hand, a second in the other, you threw the bundles into a marriage of their fluffy oats' heads, joining them in matrimony at your kneecap, withdrew your leg, and slapped another two together, then another two, followed by a seventh which you splayed out like a cap on top of the shock, to keep the oats protected from the rain while it cured. The phalanxes of shocks, in a string like a flock of geese, dotted the fields for a week or a month, depending upon when the thrashers arrived.

We kept a wary, amused eye upon the neighbors' progress in grain-cutting. Some started too soon, when the oats was pale yellow; others trusted their luck too far and let their grain lodge. The first farmer to have his fields entirely set up in shocks hoped he'd be thrashed out first. Uncle Jack announced a Thrashers' Meeting a week before the earliest neighbor would be ready for the crew. For years Jack had done custom-thrashing in the neighborhood and told tall tales of steam-powered thrashing machines belching black smoke. Now he owned a modern, sheet-metal dinosaur, the biggest around, and hauled the thrasher from farm to farm with the Grey tractor, also a curiosity, for its rear wheels were in the form of a gigantic drum with cleats to dig into the ground. The rate of pay for thrashing the neighbors' fields was geared to the number of acres done—not a money-making proposition, but the cost of gasoline and repairs was covered, and Jack had the fun of legitimately spending all his working hours with problems of motors and moving

mechanical parts, a man-made world, one up from the abject
condition of the farmer prostrate before Nature's whims.

When Jack said, "Let's call the Thrashers' Meeting for Thurs-
day," Lizzie cranked the party rings she knew so well: a long
and one short for this neighbor; two shorts and a long for that
one, and for the farthest away, she had to bring in Central.
She called into the wall phone, the black mouthpiece reaching
down to her (she was only five feet two), shouting the news
and hearing the faraway expected response, because no matter
what social event a neighbor may have planned, the Thrashers'
Meeting took precedence by authority of the season, which
would come on in its own way. Nature was a law unto itself,
and now I think it was a comfort to have one such unarguable
absolute in our lives, though then it seemed a tyranny.

We recognized each head-lamp-glowing car as it turned into
our road gate: "That's the Millers'," or, "Here come the Borms!"
Man and wife but never children, the sexes separating at the
porch door or even at the lawn gate. The men wore clean dark
blue or pin-striped overalls; their red faces and white scalps
looked scrubbed and raw—hair flattened and mousy from having been crushed under a sweaty straw hat all day. They sank
down in the cool, dew-wet grass just beyond the screened-in
porch. Here they'd smoke cigarettes and pipes without offending
us (knowing that for generations no smokers inhabited our
house, though we had handy, for courtesy, a miniature tractor
tire with a glass ashtray hub). The women found places on the
squeaky porch swing or in the rockers, and talk was amiable
but tentative.

Farmers' voices are soft from little use, often high pitched,
lines seem thrown away, for they're disdainful of the worth of
speech. What could well-chosen language do about the weather
or the price of hogs? Talk is edged with irony, amusement
over greed exposed, self-important cleverness that didn't pan
out, braggarts who got what they deserved—laughing at people,
but an oblique mockery of themselves as well: what sorry,
ridiculous lives, unseemly hopes and outrageous expectations!

Jack liked tales of steam-thrashing days. Sleepy Jesus Hansen earned his nickname because every other word uttered was "Jesus!" and because he was narcoleptic. Fell asleep even while pitching bundles into the separator of the thrashing machine and nearly got chopped up by the knives. "And then one night when the oldest Zink boy married, Sleepy Jesus and two cronies from that steam-thrashing crew spent the night drinking beer— celebrating, chivareeing the couple. Got to be two o'clock in the morning, just the hour to start stoking up the steam engine so it'd be ready to go by seven-thirty. On the way home they figured they'd better pick up the coal wagon and haul it to the steam engine. They put Sleepy Jesus in back on top of the coal. Next morning, I kept seeing these hunks of coal on the road, every little way, and I couldn't figure it out. Thought maybe the endgate fell out and they lost the coal *that* way. But when I found out Sleepy had been on the coal wagon, *then* I knew what'd happened. He kept feeling a piece of coal, hard under his back, or digging into a rib, and he'd reach under, in his sleep, and chuck it out, then move over and get rid of another lump, then another—right over the side. No wonder the wagon was pret' near empty when they got to the steam engine!" The men laughed though they'd heard the tale half a dozen times. Surrounding yourself with the old stories helped prepare the way for this year's thrashing.

Meanwhile, on the screened-in porch, a piazza which ran along half the house and around a corner, the wives talked about canning, preserving, children, and chickens. Mother and Aunt Lizzie felt a trifle uneasy, for this was the only night of the year when our visitors were other than relatives. With so many dozens of kin on both sides of the family, we needed no further friends. Religion, politics, schools were all potentially dangerous topics, but the weather and garden crops were safe. Out of boredom some visitor would lapse into gossip, and every honeyed voice in the dark urged her on. *She* knew what had caused the rift in the Knorr family—all about it. When the old man died, he left his widow only a piece of the home place, forty acres, with the stipulation that after her death the land could be bought by any of the four sons. But one son immediately bid to buy out the others and spoke for the old lady's forty as well. She gave up, hoping some relative would take her in, but her daughter said over the party line, "I'll be God-damned if *I'll* have her!"

Cluckings, murmurings on the porch swing. "Well, she wasn't wanted by any of 'em, and you know *that's* what finished her off." Open assent from all—the funeral was only last week.

These morality tales needed to be voiced and stamped into history to hold up our society. The worst thing possible for any family would be to have its reputation sullied, because like a ruptured maidenhead, it couldn't be made whole. Pregnancies out of wedlock, cruelties among relatives, arrests for drunk mayhem, any tangle with the law: these scandals revealed weaknesses hitherto unsuspected. Events over the years were recorded in the vast book of community memory, a never-ending and never-blotted chronicle. We were there too, but our family page was white and gold as yet. Nobody had found us out in a flaw, and we were determined they wouldn't.

Many of the neighbors had no such lofty notions of themselves, particularly the Catholics, for they readily confessed to the priests each week, verbalizing their wickednesses, and to speak aloud of these things was to admit they were true. The Catholics were always forgiven by the voice behind the dark cloth of the confessional—and fell into the same sinful ways all over again. But we Protestants faced our God alone, in our hearts. We were admonished by the minister not to partake of the communion unless we were sure that we were heartily sorry for our sins. The creed was spoken unanimously: "I, a poor, miserable sinner, confess unto Thee that I am by nature slothful and unclean, and that I have sinned against Thee in thought, word, and deed." In this general confession only each communicant could ascertain in what ways the words applied to him. We took the wine and wafer in our individual mouths, knowing that, if indeed we hadn't truly repented, we'd be asking for remission of sins without having a pure heart—punishment, eternal damnation. It was something each of us was responsible for. The minister fixed us with a hard, Holy Ghost look, so that we'd be sure to be honest with ourselves, doubting that we actually *were;* silently reminding us of how truly serious this was. The Catholics might fear an occasional scolding from the priest, but they never had to look God in the eye, the way we did.

On the lawn we kids would sit among the whales of men. Jack and each of his two cousins, who owned farms in our ring, weighed over two hundred and twenty pounds. There was a certain triumph in being a mountainous man, and I had these models of what I'd look like myself eventually, I hoped. Young men started toward the big gut early, right after marriage, as if the "running around" beforehand had kept them lean. They achieved their huge proportions (their wives complimented on having helped do it) and stayed that way the rest of their lives. Farm animals respected men of ample size—a well-known fact.

In the dark grass, cats would keep their distance if they sensed they were unwanted, otherwise they'd jump upon an overalled stomach mound, like a tree stump, or walk up and down the great beast-backs. Our collie was excited by the novelty of having these grown men down on a level with him, right in his territory, and he'd prowl around licking faces if anybody'd let him. The wind soughed in the big cottonwoods and whistled in the pines, as if the trees existed to give the wind a sound. Now and then a star fell, a brief, unreal streak, like God scratching on the pane of the universe.

"Well, are you guys ready for a little refreshment?" Lizzie would call, voice bantering and cheerful. She loved having this odd collection of people here and could scarcely resist preparing more than the carefully modest lemonade-and-cake we always served at Thrashers' Meeting. Too much, and these neighbor-wives would feel vaguely beholden, wonder if they should entertain us back. But the social lines were set: they had their beer-drinking card parties, their own rowdy crowd among whom they were comfortable, just as we obviously preferred to be by our Lutheran selves, with only visiting family for society. But sometimes after Jack and Lizzie, out of friendliness, attended a

wedding shower or Catholic wedding dance, they came home
flushed and excited and seemed to wonder if they should justify
the unexpected fun they'd had—to the ghost of puritanical
Grandfather lurking at the top of the stairs.

With two hostesses, Mother as well as Lizzie, no guest need
even help pass out the green tole, rectangular trays, easily dis-
tributed among the men where they lay. The lemonade was
always double strength, blended with a few oranges for color
and flavor contrast. The cakes were burnt sugar with walnuts
on the cooked frosting, or devil's food, with a white Napoleon-
style topping, tracings of bitter chocolate on the crust. These
confections were Lizzie's specialties, recipes modified and per-
fected over the years, and now her trademark—along with the
high, dozen-egg-whites angel food cakes. They were always just
right, for no mistakes were tolerated in baking anymore than
in human behavior. Everyone—and everything—had an expected
role to play: the eggs, butter, sugar, milk were to blend, the
oven was to heat properly, the cakes were to rise, and the
timer was to ring when it should. Though there were so many
uncertain areas in a farmer's life, about which he might be helpless and unable to exert control, some things—a cake perforce—
must be made to come out absolutely flawless.

Not until a man yawned or pulled a pocket watch from his
fob, squinting in the moonlight to read it, did Jack finally,
agonizingly ask, "Well, who's going to be first this year?" In
fact, every farmer secretly wanted to be thrashed out first—
have his oats safely stashed in granary bins—but courtesy held
their tongues. Backtracking all the way, only under Jack's direct
questioning did someone finally admit that yes, his oats would
probably be all set up in shocks by next Wednesday, eighty
acres—two thrashing days. On Friday, Jack would move the
rig to the second farm on the list. Catholics knew that by rights
it should be one of them, so that a Protestant housewife wouldn't
have to provide fish for the whole bunch. These schedules often
went wrong because of rain and postponements—and then,
what private complaining! How ridiculous that on one day of
the week Catholics *had* to have tuna-fish sandwiches, and for

the main meal salmon loaf. In truth, the priests gave harvest dispensations, and the Catholic harvesters *could* eat meat on Friday if Protestant hosts set out nothing else. But we were courteous, careful neighbors and didn't want trouble over such a trifle. Meat and fish were served in platters side by side, and surprisingly, often as a gesture of good will, Catholic thrashers would take meat instead of fish, and Protestants would return the compliment by eating fish. August 15, the day of the Assumption of the Virgin, was another matter; not a Catholic would work on such a holy day, and invariably the weather was sunny and dry, perfect for thrashing. Protestants would sit home and curse the Pope.

At last the exact order of thrashing was set, and very soon afterward the men rose in the dark, like buffaloes at a watering hole, and lumbered off toward their cars. The women on the porch made their farewells in high, false voices and followed. Lizzie never knew until the last guest had gone just when *we* were to have the thrashers but figured that, as usual, Jack would allow everyone else to have first choice, then take what was left. We were almost always last. He preferred to risk grain loss for the good will engendered—it was *his* ring, and he was the grain harvest host.

The summer I was eleven I joined the thrashing crew as blower tender. After the season, I knew Jack would remember me with a special treat in entertainment, clothes, or cash, but I wasn't assigned this job for pay; rather, it was expected of me: that it was time I made a more significant work contribution to the family than just the daily chicken chores, scything, weed-pulling, and gardening. As a thrasher, I was catered to at our home table in a totally different way, served and fed as if my time were important, my energies vital; the women were to surround me with a workman's necessities. Away, however, in the eyes of the crew, I was a kid of no consequence, somebody to tease in an idle hour as they waited in the shade of the bundle racks to unload at the machine.

Everyone knew Jack didn't allow drinking on this crew, but some of the hired men sneaked along beer bottles and I tasted my first: the wicked ambrosial stuff that caused the famous troubles—girls laid when they didn't know what they were doing, guys killed, too drunk to drive. So this was the fabled drink! A flat, galvanized, metallic edge—horrible tasting. The men laughed when I spit it out in disgust. They also kidded me when I turned my back to pee on a rear wheel, saying I ought to put chickenshit on it to make it grow. They told raunchy stories I didn't understand.

Each morning Jack maneuvered the great sheet-metal thrasher into position away from the wind, so that the chaff from the blower wouldn't settle back on top of us all. The farmer himself indicated where he wished the strawstack created, usually in a cattle lot near the barn, but sometimes in a bin of the barn, in which case I'd aim the coughing blower spout directly into a barn window. Inside, some poor stacker would half suffocate as he spread the straw around. Occasionally the strawstack would be blown in a corner of a stubble field, too far away to be used up in winter bedding for stalls; these stacks barely lasted the winter as outdoor cattle shelters and food for them.

Two bundle racks worked together, since the feeder of the thrashing machine was filled from two sides. Each farmer fielded at least one rack, two if he'd planted a great deal of grain. In the morning, with the dew heavy on the sheaves, the earliest racks couldn't begin picking up their loads until seven-thirty or eight. Jack had time to oil the thrasher, unroll the belt (which he made into an elongated figure eight), one end around the drive wheel of the Grey tractor, the other attached to the master shaft of the thrasher.

Tending blower took little skill but a great deal of attention. The tube could be extended like a telescope. I sat on a little wooden platform with this enormous thing between my legs, no chickenshit needed at all, and it spewed stuff all over the place. One wheel controlled the left-right direction, and I could swing the blower about ninety degrees; another wheel determined the length of the tube, short at the beginning when we were just starting a stack, and all the way out, as far as it could reach, when we were nearly finished. A rope guided the hood of the blower, which deflected the straw stream, crimping it to fall straight down, or allowing the gobs full leeway to arch high in the air. The stacker signaled to me just what he wanted—a wave to left or right, pointing with his finger, flapping his hands open or shut, imitating the mouth of the blower, making these hand signals quickly, scarcely looking up, for the chaff would litter his eyes if he opened them too wide. As I got used to my job, he scarcely had to tell me where to blow the straw. I'd move the stuff around and out of his way, while he neatly stacked with the pitchfork, spreading the fluffy golden straw, waist deep in it, building the corners strong, tamping it down—but like dream-walking, scarcely getting anywhere. He'd come around under the blower spout, while I swung it over the spot where he'd just been, creating layers this way, lifting him up, off the ground, until finally he'd never have been able to get down to the ground if someone hadn't brought a ladder.

Most stackers were men who enjoyed the artistic challenge of creating a strong, beautiful stack and didn't too much mind chaff blowing down their necks. The stacker had to be provided by the farmer being thrashed out: sometimes it was a relative who now lived in town but liked to rally round at thrashing time in the country, imbibing the atmosphere of men and grain and fields, feeling nostalgic about his childhood. My beefy cousin Ross, mayor of the nearby town, was one of these stackers, and he was kept busy among his relatives in our thrashing ring. Dressed in clean-from-the-store overalls, he hunkered down with the thrashers at lunch hour, told stories and chewed oats' straws—what great fun! Loved those huge thrasher noon meals, too, and kidding the ladies in the kitchen (he was a bachelor). They knew his reputation for packing away food and loved him for it; he'd once won the sweet corn-eating contest and the pile of cobs on the platter in front of him rose so high it nearly hid his fat red face. Ross specialized in strawstacks shaped like large loaves of bread. Uncle Jack was a skilled stacker, too, and often did ours in the shape of a half-moon, like the almond crescent cookies we had at Christmas.

Probably only an eleven-year-old boy could have stood the awful shaking I got, from eight in the morning until seven-thirty at night, when the dew came back and we had to stop. What a tremendous upheaval going on in the guts of that thrasher! Knives slashed the binder twine holding the sheaves, the stalks were shaken and shifted, heads violently knocked, the seeds loosened; and great shuttling sieve pans would go to work until the seeds, heavier than straw and chaff, fell into a pit, where the grain auger lifted them up and roweled them out a spout and into the waiting grain wagon, while the straw stalks were heaved with great force through the blower. Hour after hour I shook all over; dust and chaff settled upon me. Only the sharpest, most piercing, calamitous cries got through to me. When at last the Grey sputtered to evening silence, and the ratcheting noises in the box I sat on began to subside like a beast dying, I was clobbered by the stillness, almost unable to hear anything. I climbed down the little iron ladder from my perch, legs terribly stiff, arms sore—to be revived by cold supper at the farmhouse, then home to bath and bed. In harvest we allowed ourselves the luxury of a bath every night and clean overalls next day, though none of the neighbors did. Their garments by the end of the week smelled as rank as their horses, each man with his characteristic, enveloping odor, some more tolerable than others—the tobacco users made the richest compound.

During those long, blower-tending hours, I studied all the men and animals and got to know well what each creature was like: the mean white-faced bay who nipped the flanks of horses and bared her teeth to the men; the sleepy mules; the tired old nags who seemed to have thoughts on earlier, green pasture years; the earnest, stolid farmers who took pride in building efficient loads and caused nobody trouble; the show-offs who did it all too fast; the harvest-season hired hands who rough-handled their teams and didn't give a damn what anybody thought of them.

One guy would devilishly set too fast a pace as he fed the machine from the top of his load. His partner on the other side of the feeder belt, tossing bundles against the bangboard divider, had to hustle or he'd find himself ignobly all alone, the quick-man having pulled away in his empty rack. The man still unloading had to pitch in bundles double time in order not to have the thrasher make a queer, racing noise, from having too little to work with. But most neighbors were considerate partners and during the two weeks paired together formed such a strong bond that even the old reserve between Protestants and Catholics fell away. Bathed in August heat, under the pale prairie sky, they'd witness each other's strongest moments and small failings, knew who could take the sun and who couldn't—they emerged physically real to each other. Unloading at the feeder, they were like a married pair and found their own rhythms, matching bundle for bundle until they were down to the bare boards at the same moment. Jack would run to lower the magneto lever on the tractor, slow down the drive belt, and the thrasher would pause to digest what it had just been through. The stacker up there could lean on his pitchfork in clean air or slump down in his tracks, hidden in the golden nest, and I'd stand for a stretch of my limbs or run to the water jug for a swig.

Before the next team drew up to the feeder, Jack would take a pitchfork and clean up the spill from the ground. Otherwise, it would soon be too deep for the wagons to come near enough. Some horses were so nervous by the moving belts and noise they refused to move close; others got their teams alongside the tilted edge of the feeder and could almost slide the top bundles onto the conveyer belt without lifting them. The horses were soon littered with chaff and looked as if they'd been in a snowstorm.

Jack had no other job than to see that the tractor and thrasher didn't break down, and if things were going smoothly, he'd relieve me at the blower now and then. I'd either rest next to the lemonade pail, which was wrapped in wet gunny sacks and placed under the shade of a wagon, and join in the men's talk—or ride the oats wagon to the granary with the old man who usually attended to such leisurely matters. One's body contours fit perfectly in the grain quicksand; it was cool and slippery, relaxing to sink into. The wagon was heavy for the horses to pull, the pace slow, and the sound of wheel squeaks was peace itself.

Since I was a fat-boy before puberty, urged to eat on, the size of me a visible reassurance that I wouldn't be whisked into death like my father, my thoughts while tending blower focused on the four meals (not counting breakfast) we ate each day. From my high perch on the thrasher I'd often be the first to spot the women in pale cotton housedresses, with small children, drawing a coaster wagon filled with the ten-o'clock lunch: a milk can of lemonade clinking with chunks of ice, an enameled gray or blue coffeepot, and hampers of sand-wiches and tins of cookies. This feeding was too insignificant to warrant stopping the thrashing machine. Ten-o'clock lunch would continue for an hour, until those men picking up bundles in the fields would all have come to the machine. Sometimes the housewives left the food and drink in a shady spot, on the running board of a parked car angled against the sun, or under an idle wagon, but usually they lingered in order to find out how the thrashing was going—was the oats running good? About how many bushels to the acre? They tried to penetrate the secrets of the thrasher's world, but none of us paid much attention or answered them seriously, since the morning lunch was their purpose in coming out here. They never even com-plained or tried to intervene if the stack we were blowing happened to be directly in line with the house. With a strong wind, chaff would cling to all the screens, litter porch floors like pollen, seep under the cracks of doors, and fill the house with debris which would take a week to clean up. Such dirty days were just bad luck for womenfolk.

Our operation shut down at noon, and the men who'd just finished at the machine would drive their empty racks into the farmyard, unhitch their teams, and lead them to the watering troughs and oats' bins in the barn. In this way the beasts of the neighborhood became acquainted with the fixtures, fare, and different farm layouts, along with their masters. Before we men could enter the strange house in our dusty, filthy clothes, we had to clean up a little, pull ourselves out of the comfortable sloth of Nature's domain and into the necessary humanizing environment of a home, where floors shone, dishes sparkled, and chairs creaked unhappily under our heavy hams. In the grassy yard just outside the farmhouse door, washstands had been set upon orange crates and towels hung from the clothesline. Mirror, comb, and brush were perched on a handy tree crotch or propped against a porch pillar. We were all expected to do our best at grooming, for our self-respect but also to pay the tribute to decency the women knew we'd wish: to present ourselves as clean as circumstances allowed, as neat-looking as we could manage. If they couldn't extract *this* effort from us, squalor and hopeless farm-inundation surely doomed us all.

In the house, shades had been severely drawn all morning, and even now they were still pulled against the fierce sun. It was orange-dim and slightly cooler here where the huge table was laid out, every available leaf put in, an oilcloth or real tablecloth over the expanse. Near the kitchen door it was noticeably warmer, for many homes still had cob-and-wood black iron cookstoves. A drape or swing door shielded the men as they dined, from this forgelike heat, which the wives had to endure; yet the women tried to look fresh in their ruffled, clean aprons and smiled as they brought in the hot food.

In Protestant homes some thrasher (or more often, a household child) sitting among us said "the blessing" aloud; in Catholic houses there was only a slight bow of the head and a quick breast-cross. Bowls and platters were passed and waitresses stood nearby to see that no man on a far end missed out on any dish. The thrashers ate silently, not much used to talking at meals even at home: the visiting could come later, after the food had been dispatched. Fried spring chicken, mashed potatoes and gravy, creamed corn, fresh tomatoes,

cucumbers in vinegar or sour milk, with onion; roast pork or
ham, beef roasts; apple pie using the sour green apples just
ready now, or fresh peach pie, or cream pies. Every meal
offered some especially tasty item, different from home fare,
but there wasn't much time to savor it, for out in the yard,
hair wetted and slicked back, more thrashers were waiting for
a place at the table. When one got up and left the dining
room, another came in. Sometimes, to simplify passing of food,
the first shift pushed back from the table at the same time,
and the second shift started their meal all together.

Logy with the heavy food, in the humid heat of an August
midday, we could scarcely do anything but drag ourselves to
the shade of an ash tree and flop down in the grass, hoping
there wasn't too much chickenshit around. For a while nobody
moved, slain by food and fatigue. Far away on a radio the
noon market report in a singsong voice like an auctioneer's reminded us that the shuttlings of the economic life held us in a
tight weave of circumstance. At last, awakened by the persistent flies, some men would sit up and read the Sioux City
Journal, but only the sports news. Pervading our somnolence,
our rest, was the resonant energy of the women chattering in the
kitchen, who spoke brightly to the men as they brought in
food, cheerful and excited, who knew how to be the courtesans
we needed at this time. They were delighted by the dinner
party, eager to show off their famous cooking, pleased to have
neighbors in the house. There wasn't a dour female bunch
in any of these houses, and their laughter and gaiety (without
our thinking much about it) cheered us on our way.

In the sole bachelor house of our thrashing ring, the thirty-
five-year-old host always got teased, asked if there was anything cooking? Or would we all have to go to a restaurant
in town—and didn't he need a woman? He batched with his
old man and they fared all right, the son being no longer even
in the market for a wife. But the thrashers had him on the run
with their dirty kidding, for a farmer who isn't fertile himself
seemed anomalous, a sport. Why was he in this business
of sexual production if he couldn't manage it himself? The

ladies of the neighborhood rallied round with more ardor and interest in their "helping out" than normally exhibited. They fell over themselves in the kitchen, figuring out the rudimentary equipment—pump in the kitchen and no electrical appliances. The cookstove was a leftover from a generation ago when the son was growing up; no housewife had been around recently to demand better. They poured feminine attention into the household, a heady syrup, to show him and all of us thrashers just what a difference they made.

When Jack reluctantly rose from the grass and knuckle-rubbed his leg muscles, which knotted up in cramps some nights so severely he had to use the bed sheets for a tourniquet to relax them (though salt tablets, which we all took, helped prevent these cramps), it was time for thrashing again. Sometimes, before beginning the afternoon's work, we'd shift the machine and start a new stack in another part of the barnyard. Whenever the wind changed we *had* to tack with it, otherwise the blower would shower us all. I got set for the long, loud afternoon, cowering under the broad brim of the straw hat as if under eaves, in the falling chaff and dust storm. If we were thrashing barley, the beards stickery as grasshopper legs would sometimes scrape down my back or, worst of all, lodge in my belly button. Only by resolutely telling myself I was a man now could I conquer the day and slowly watch the hot sun descend —wondering all along just what time it was, thinking of the four-o'clock lunch oasis. If only I could endure this awful noise and shaking until then.

At last I sighted the afternoon refreshments: an unaccounted-for automobile driving out a gate of the grove; or the lunch would arrive again by a kid pulling a coaster wagon. Sometimes the host-farmer himself would drive to the house and pick up the dishpans full of store-bought white bread sandwiches, buttered and filled with thinly sliced bologna, and cream cans of lemonade with iceberg chunks which had been bought in town. Jack would shut down the big Grey, and while the harvesters gathered in the sun to drink lemonade out of enameled cups or cheap glasses, or coffee from white porcelain mugs (some farmers drank only hot liquids in hot weather), he'd busily squirt his oil can at every socket he could find, crawl all over his lovable, warm thrashing machine, reassuring the monster that it was doing fine. The stacks of sandwiches under the dishcloths (hidden from the horseflies) quickly disappeared. Although every farmer's wife baked bread once a week, it was big-holed and often soured in summer after a few days—it was only for family consumption. Everyone preferred the cottony grocer's bread, which stayed so fresh and wadded up into nothing. We ate the sandwiches, cookies, and cakes without washing our hands, stoking ourselves quickly; it was hardly even a rest.

Then, three more hours. With great excitement I felt the cooling breeze which blew low to the ground steal up my bare legs, announcing evening—and the dew which would rescue me from this ordeal. "Yours'll be the last loads—you two guys," Jack would shout to a pair pulling away from the machine. With a grin the farmers would rattle off in their empty hayracks, slapping the horses' rumps with the reins— cheered to realize that tomorrow they could sleep a bit later, for they'd be at the end of the cycle. Wouldn't have to begin pitching bundles until nearly nine o'clock, even though tonight they'd be awfully tired, the very last ones home.

The final thrasher's meal was a cold supper in the house, platters of "lunch meat," potato salad, sliced tomatoes, pickles, and whatever cakes and pies were still left after a day's feasting (always more held in reserve), and sometimes, especially at our house, a scoop of vanilla ice cream on apple pie. A few thrashers bypassed the supper, without giving offense, eager to return home to chores awaiting them: herds to milk and pigs to feed. Animal demands always took precedence over one's comfort or obligations to a host. In later years, because some wives said the evening supper was one meal too many, it was decided at a Thrashers' Meeting to have no more of them. That was just the first of the curtailments, which would eventually end with a decision not to thrash at all.

Jack worked long after everyone else had gone to the farmhouse for supper. He yanked the huge belt from the tractor drive wheel and laid it out on the stubble, like a ribbon divider on a highway, then rolled it into a tight shell-like coil, to be stashed away under tarpaulin for the night. Next came the smaller belts that drove the secondary shafts in the thrasher. He folded up the canvas, slatted conveyer belt of the feeder so that it wouldn't be spoiled by night moisture. He knew which panels could be screwed off, allowing him to crawl right into the machine itself, like Jonah, and roam around in there, feeling his way in the dark, knowing every sharp, metallic moving part as well as the ribs and sinews of his body.

I'd wait on the running board of the car until he was done. Or, if this day's thrashing finished off the farmer's oats fields, he'd further dismantle the machine, push the blower all the way into itself, and rest it on top of the machine, like a duck with head under its wing. The grain spout would be swung around and secured with a rope; it nestled in wooden resting loops along the top rim. After the feeder became detached, a tongue in front of the thrasher made hitching it to the tractor possible—the feeder was attached to the very end, like a caboose. Then with a grunt the tractor, which had been diverted in its power all day (merely throwing its drive wheel, not turning its wheels), got the chance to heave forward, lugs digging into the turf, feeling all its mechanical muscles at once in the relief of movement. Jack was off! To pull into the farmyard of tomorrow's thrashing scene, where his equipment would be left overnight. I'd follow in the car, able to reach the clutch with a good stretch of my toes, if I sat on the edge of the plush seat. On the way home I'd relinquish the driver's wheel to him, for I was technically too young to drive and had no license.

After a couple of years a different boy of the neighborhood was hired to tend blower, since I was needed to steer our truck, which had a bundle rack attached to the back. Our horses were too old to do anything but pull the grain wagon back and forth from the thrashing machine to the granary. I piloted the truck rack for whomever Jack hired for the season

—his son, who earned college money; my two older brothers, and once a high school basketball star, who hoped to keep himself in shape. Soon I was in charge of this rack myself, with a boy driver to order around.

I'd dig into a side of the shock with my pitchfork, catching two or three bundles by the twine. Field mice scurried in all directions, occasionally a startled Jack rabbit fled. To build a load properly took a mason's skill, for the butts were all laid bottoms out, row after row, with the hollow center of the rack filled up now and then for inner support. Since the front and rear of the wagon were high with boards, you had only to worry about the sides, which had to be mosaic-laid strongly enough to prevent the whole thing from sliding away on the jouncy trip to the machine. If you lost part of your load, nothing of it could be salvaged; you simply had to throw the bundles off your rack and start all over again, for straw stalks were slippery. Show-offs would build a huge, balanced head, neat as a boy's dome in a barber chair. The final pitching up to the top took considerable strength, for you had to fix the pitchfork into the bundle just right so that when you heaved it up in a wide arc over your shoulder it would land in the exact place you intended. You always worked away from the wind, using its force when you could; and you had to eye your partner's progress in order to keep up with him. When I first started, a spike pitcher sometimes helped me out, otherwise the machine would have been ready for me, my partner waiting at the feeder, but I'd still be out in the field. Spike pitchers roamed the stubble fields helping slowpokes— a thankless job, since they never could rest and even missed out on the midmorning and midafternoon lunches.

Thrashing stopped just as my childhood ended: the war came, hired men found assembly-line factory jobs or were drafted; the older boys in my family enlisted. Farmers had to rely on machinery to do their work, not human muscles and animal strength. Although Jack hated to admit it, the contest between the virtues of the grain combine and the thrasher had been won by the combine. A farmer "got through" in a single operation—reaping, threshing all took place at once. But you don't have a strawstack! my uncle objected. A combine merely ejected the loose straw onto the field and a baler had to come and pick it up. What farmer didn't need a strawstack to provide winter bedding in hog pens and chicken barns?

Well, with bales of straw stored in the barn, one had compact lozenges which could be broken open all winter—plenty of straw for bedding. There was much waste in a strawstack: the tops spoiled in wet weather and rotten pockets developed in the best stacks. Pigs in a yard would often undermine strawstacks so severely they toppled over, sometimes with the animals underneath, suffocating. Finally the arguments stopped—none of the neighbors wanted Jack to thrash for them. They'd all made combine arrangements. Finally, *he* did too, and bought a half interest in a secondhand combine, with a neighbor-cousin. Now the annual small grain harvest was as routine as corn picking.

For fun, he converted the thrashing machine into a gawky, elephantine combine. It was so weird to see the monstrous thing moving through an oats field—a thrasher that had lost its way—farmers driving by on the road nearly lost control of their cars. But the converted contraption worked! The county newspaper sent a photographer, wrote a feature story, and finally a television crew came out from Sioux City. This thrashing machine refused to die: it beat the wheel of progress in agronomy, found a way of *not* going the route of horses into oblivion. Like all species saved from extinction, Jack knew how to adapt—so that both he and the thrasher could live on.

What's missed, however, I know for not being out there anymore, smelling the nutty, farina odor of oats blown into a granary. No more gathering in of sheaves, neighbors together for their yearly harvest communion, ceremony without articulation. The grave courtesy of country people among themselves arose out of a recognition of what their stopped tongues did not have to say. With baleful, aware eyes they peered around the orb of this annual experience, knowing it was the time of their full earthly season. The thrasher's ring was also the circle of their days.

There's a sad triumph in the gathering of sheaves—filling the empty granaries, successfully preventing the seeds from reaching the soil. We captured those grain heads thick with seeds, millions and millions of them, numerous as the sperm we ourselves produced constantly and wasted. Another year of the soil's fertility pushed to this orgiastic climax, then a falling away to somnolence and snow.

And for what? The small-grain harvest was often our cash crop, coming in summer when the money was badly needed, but the dollars were soon spent; or the oats were consumed by the livestock in a few months, and *they* were sold on the market. Never a stopping moment, never a time when one had truly secured the future, provided enough, worked hard enough. I remember being appalled when I first learned the futility of the relentless seasons. *Why, why,* I asked, must I pull these weeds from the garden, when more of them will surely grow tomorrow? The query was too unsettling for my elders, too profound.

They laughed and couldn't answer me.

9.   Father, Forgive Them

If we traveled beyond the sanctuary of our farm in 1932 and 1933, the automobile might be stopped by men waving pitch-forks. Uncle Jack would try to smile and familiarly called out their names, to weaken their unfriendliness. When the farm strikers saw the interior piled deep with children, not egg crates and cream cans, they dropped back into the ditch weeds. We rode past cars with trunks open for inspection and rear seats jerked out of place. The Farmers' Holiday picketeers were searching for produce that might reach market in defiance of their embargo. Creeks were cloudy with dumped milk cans and thousands of smashed eggs coated the roadside grass, at these checkpoints. What fun the farmers had doing it—like children playing hooky, on holiday from serious farm work. Mother and Aunt Lizzie deplored the confiscations, for what right had these men to use force—even if they thought their cause was just? And Uncle Jack agreed. "They keep this up and they'll land in the clink." But the sheriff did nothing to break up the barri-cades, and the strike was on.

At home we played Farmers' Holiday on the sidewalk, upend-ing the coaster wagon and scooter, building a barrier to stop traffic. One of us would try to run the blockade, but he'd be caught and threatened with a beating unless he turned around and went back. Perhaps he'd be ambushed near a spiraea bush, stopped by picketeers carrying lathe swords. Strikers or scabs, which was it best to be?

Just before school started, Mother took me to the shoe store in town. Following barefoot summer days, the new shoes were like hasps on my feet, but in their tissue wrappings, how good they smelled! Mr. Lucas's shop was across the street from the Toy bank, where we kept our money. Mr. Toy's chain of banks were the only ones around that hadn't gone into receivership, being better managed than the name would indicate. Our bank was next to the grocer's, where we traded because he belonged to our church. "You know, *they're* over there," said Mr. Lucas gravely, nodding toward the store.

"That bunch again?" Mother said, pursing her lips. I'd noticed a knot of overalled farmers milling about strangely on Main Street. "Well, they're not after shoes. And you don't have any eggs, Mr. Lucas, so I guess they won't come in here to smash things up."

"What should we do?" I asked, alarmed by the sudden alertness in Mother's manner and the way she turned to peer out the large window, which was halfway covered by café curtains.

"They'll be soon gone," Mr. Lucas murmured, trying to smile casually, but like all town tradesmen, he was terrified by the drift of lawlessness. Raids on grocery stores occurred at any hour. They'd break into refrigerator compartments and remove produce farmers had bartered for flour, salt, and sugar. The town marshal, a onetime farmer himself, seemed helpless before them, for he was a poolroom friend of them all. Mother believed in law and was determined to avoid showing fright, not only out of conviction, but as a proper example to me. When Mr. Lucas had finished wrapping the shoe box, we left the shop as if nothing out of the ordinary were happening.

A dozen men loitered on the sidewalk across the street, poles, baseball bats, and shotguns in their hands. A tall, unshaven farmer in dirty striped overalls stepped out of the grocer's, head high. Lazily, he lifted his arm. "Come on, boys, this way!"

They followed him slowly down the street to the next food store. As far as I could see in either direction, the entire town was deserted, except for them.

"Do you know him, Mother? Who is he?" I climbed upon the running board and stepped into the car.

Aunt Lizzie spoke immediately to her sister: "Wasn't *that* something? In broad daylight, just doing what they please. It's a wonder they don't try robbing the bank."

But what aroused Mother's indignation was that the overalled ringleader had looked right at her without a flicker of recognition, as if he'd never seen her before. "I should've called, 'John, what are you doing?'"

"They're going pretty far, I'd say," Lizzie half-smiled in her disapproval, for we youngsters weren't to think that the reliable world was close to collapse or already gone entirely.

"Roosevelt had *better* be elected!" Mother said. We'd always voted Republican, but now Hoover's name filled us with loathing.

"Who *was* that man, *John?*" I wanted to know. They told me, but not until years later did I place him in the enormous family tree we sometimes constructed for our amusement as we sat on the screened-in porch and watched the moon's progress toward the west. Tired of pointing out strange figures in the clouds, playing guessing-animals, or having dredged up all the poetry of Longfellow or Whittier anybody knew, we began "the relations game." The trick was to name somebody—any of the two or three thousand people in our community—and build a relationship between that person and us. Newcomers couldn't be suggested, for unless there'd been time to intermarry and produce children, he couldn't be related to us. My maternal grandfather had had three wives—my paternal grandfather's family had been prolific, and hence the routes to community kinships were numerous. Now with the bearded ringleader, John, it was simple: he was connected to the Meier family on his mother's side and related to the Ammons' clan, one of whose numbers had married the daughter of Mother's stepsister. So, John was pretty close kin. "And to think, he's gotten so big-headed he pretends he doesn't recognize you anymore!" said Mother.

Our family had a Farmers' Holiday member—August, who was married to Mother's favorite stepsister. One day his black Buick sped into our road gate and came to a sharp halt. Laddie barked while dust in great clouds settled through the trees slowly—the soft comment of the inanimate world, which I noticed in conjunction with flailing human activity, but about which at the age of six I could not speak.

August's Jack-in-the-box eyes were rolling wildly. "Sure I saw the guns but I never thought they meant it!" voice oiled and resonant, even in his excitement.

"You better watch out you don't get *killed,*" said Lizzie, standing at the gatepost, sister-to-brother in her reprimand, deeply concerned and knowing she must speak. "Running around the countryside this way, what do you expect?"

Behind the adults, on the lawn under the mock-orange bush, we caught the tremor of alarm and watched Uncle Jack seriously inspect the rear of the car. The older boys crowded close. "Look—look, here's where the bullet went in!"

"But where did it come out?"

"Isn't the upholstery torn anywhere?"

"No, see—the window was open."

"But if it went in right *here,* it must've landed *some*place!"

August paced up and down, laughing nervously, proud of what he'd been through. Helped by a band of vigilantes, a grocer in a neighboring town had opened fire on August and other Holidayers when they tried to raid his store. "Those law-and-order boys can't shoot too good!" His old, infectious giggle erupted, white teeth flashing.

I stole out of the play lot to have a closer look at the rear of the Buick. I asked a brother to lift me up, so I could put my finger into the jagged bullet hole. "Don't!" shouted Mother. "He'll cut himself. What are you boys doing? Put him down."

I wasn't supposed to catch on to any of this, wasn't to lose my innocence. Let violence come to me when nothing more could be done to stop it. For up to now, terror was held just behind the closed door, if possible. We were to remain secure from fears of disaster. And yet we heard about the chicken thief whose head was blasted off by a rigged shotgun placed over the barn door. A bankrupt farmer a mile down the road stuck a vacuum cleaner hose into his car's exhaust pipe and closed the garage door on himself. My cousin's drunken husband attacked her with a broken catsup bottle when he learned she was pregnant for the fourth time. And gory tales abounded of mangled hands in corn pickers and limbs torn off in highway accidents.

Mother tried to create an atmosphere of order and safety to counterbalance all of this, just as the Devil might be acknowledged but never paid tribute to. We were not to have nightmares over Dillinger or Al Capone, though the Lindbergh kidnaping *did* upset us until convinced we were too poor to be snatched from our beds. We never discussed my dead father because of the harm it might do us. After all, why think about him, since we had Uncle Jack for a father now? But a clock in our house had stopped on the exact minute of his death; that eerie occurrence was accidentally mentioned *once,* then hushed up. Since I was a baby when he died of pneumonia (or was it a bad heart?), the details remained vague. He'd worked "altogether too hard," Mother often said. Farm work could kill you, and *that* was another good reason why our eyes must be on the horizon, where the cities lay.

I felt the raw, sharp edges of the bullet hole with keen interest but not much awe. I already knew all about this sweet life-and-death game everyone played. Stalking animals and birds was the most thrilling activity of an older boy's life. I'd seen the glassy-eyed, bleeding rabbits on the back floor of the Model A Ford, after we'd shot them on the run from our bouncing vehicle, in midnight hunts across the stubble fields of the Eighty. It was a day of luck when Jack returned with plump, dangling pheasants —the gorgeous feathers always hid the fatal wounds. And the pious remark that they were really too beautiful to shoot never came across seriously. After the quick crack of the rifle shot, I'd watch the russet tree squirrel fall with legs outspread—half-flying—making a thud on the ground like a dropped apple. All this wild flesh was meant for our table. We'd pick out the bee-bees from the pheasant meat and roll them with a tinkle on our plates.

The bullet hole was no surprise: I had my finger stuck at last into the times.

"Pretty Boy" Floyd sounded like a playmate I might know, and banks nearby were being robbed in broad daylight: "This is a stick-up," the words still new, the fresh language of terror. Uncle Jack's cousin knew the man who'd shot Jesse James. "Shot him in the back in St. Joseph, Missouri." Yes, the assassin, Ford, was undoubtedly a coward, as everyone said, but wasn't it interesting to know the man who'd done such a famous deed? "Had to shoot Jesse James in the back," Jack smiled, admiringly, " 'cause that's the *only* way Jesse James could've been taken."

I hoped for minor criminals such as chicken thieves to visit our farm, for the henhouses were somewhat near the road. We trusted Laddie to keep the night watch, though sometimes he raised a midnight fuss over a rabbit in the woodpile. I'd lie awake nights trying to hear the rustle of thieves in the grove, but it was always only the wind; or I'd scrutinize the dark from my upstairs bedroom window and try to catch a glimpse of a flashlight among the trees. I'd listen for the muffled squawks of captured hens in gunny sacks, knowing exactly how the thieves would proceed: after blinding a sleepy chicken with a flashlight beam, they'd catch her scaly yellow legs in a long, loop-end rod, whisk her off the roost, and fling her head-first into the sack—as I'd seen Uncle Jack do when he caught a bunch for market. But despite all my watching, no chicken thieves came.

"If you think times are bad *now*," some adult would say—erasing the portentous present by conjuring up the dangerous past.

Aunt Elizabeth, for instance, had dealt with a menacing cut-throat of the Dakotas—singlehanded. She taught school in Pierre, South Dakota, at the turn of the century, and one spring she rode with her pupils on a spring outing to the bluffs overlooking the Missouri River. After tying their mounts to the trees, they began fixing their picnic lunch. Soon a strange man on a black horse came galloping toward them. "Oh, such a huge, rough character! And he didn't smile or greet us in any way, just went to the children and began tying their hands behind their backs. I didn't know what he planned to do, steal our horses, rob me—but I didn't even feel afraid, because he made me so darn mad! Spoiling our picnic this way! I just grabbed the big butcher knife I had with me and cut the bindings of the oldest boy. And then I turned to the outlaw, pointing with my knife: 'Now you just get out of here as fast as you can, if you know what's good for you!' "

And then what happened? What did he do?

"Why, he leapt on his horse and rode away. I scared him off!"

Mother, tell about the train robber.

In 1908 when she was only eighteen, she journeyed by train sixty miles to a one-room country schoolhouse where she had her first job. Suddenly in the next coach, shots were fired. A man shouted, "Train robber! Train robber! Everybody down on the floor!" She scrooched below the seat but peeped in the aisle and through the open, swaying doors between carriages saw the masked bandit, hat low on his forehead, gun glittering in his hand. He searched through women's purses, dropped all money, watches, jewelry into a small white bag used for coin deposits in banks. Mother stuffed her cash and gold watch under the green plush cushion, but before the robber entered her coach, the train began to slow for a town. He got nervous and leapt from the open platform into a clump of brush. "No, he was never caught. Train robberies were common in those days. But all that's past history," she'd say with a reassuring smile. "You kids have never even *been* on a train yet, have you? One of these days we'll put you on for a short ride and meet you in the next town. Just for the fun of it." Also, we had to have some experience in traveling in order to make the big journeys away she had in mind for us.

Uncle Jack sympathized with the Farmers' Holiday aims and had long championed the farm co-operative movement in the

grain-elevator business, but he didn't join the Farmers' Union
or the Farmers' Holiday because strike tactics offended his sense
of orderly, law-abiding good-citizenship, which he'd inherited
so strongly from Grandfather. "They come around and want
your dollar for membership, but what does a fellow get for
that dollar? You only help these guys run around the countryside
in their cars, burning up gas." Although farmers traditionally
joined forces to help in harvest, he couldn't see them acting
together to change the economy. Nor did he believe that with-
holding produce from the market would force prices up. "Don't
you know, the market's rigged somewhere along the line, and
no bunch of farmers is going to figure out how it's done!"

On the day Judge Bradley was nearly hanged, Uncle Jack,
who knew nothing about the rioting in the county seat town
eleven miles away, drove to the medical clinic for a prescrip-
tion; one of us was sick. He walked up the creaky stairs and
asked the switchboard girl, Irene, "Where *is* everybody?" He
was dressed in overalls and hadn't shaved for two or three days.
Irene's eyes widened and she sat there rigid, without answering.
"I didn't know what was the matter, so I finally said I wanted
that medicine I'd come for—and I needed it in a hurry. And
boy, did she run for it fast! Why, *that* must've been just after
they'd dragged out the judge! If I'd gone to town by the country
road instead of the pavement, I'd've seen the mob. I guess Irene
thought I was going to wreck the place, I looked so tough!"

Next day we stayed home from school because National Guard
trucks were traveling muddy country roads, looking for rebels.
Each time the phone rang, no matter what the party ring,
Mother or Lizzie took down the receiver and "rubbered." Listening for news, who'd been caught, who the soldiers were still
looking for. No, stepbrother August hadn't been involved, thank
God!

The last thing Judge Bradley reportedly said, before the noose
strangled him unconscious, was "Father, forgive them, for they
know not what they do." It was three o'clock on a Friday afternoon, but not Good Friday—Easter had been celebrated weeks
before. Prior to stringing him up on a light pole, the farmers

had stripped off his trousers and underwear and daubed his testicles with axle grease from a hubcap. Pulling out a knife, they threatened castration. They meant to scare him, not kill him, and Bradley did not die.

"To think they'd do something like *that* to Judge Bradley! A man in *his* position," said Mother. She became acquainted with the judge because Father died intestate, and the court had appointed her guardian. Under state law she received the widow's one-third of the estate, and we had the rest, which she administered. Periodically, accompanied by her lawyer, she went to the courthouse "to give an accounting of her expenditures." Her sense of dignity was somewhat offended by the proceeding: to have family business made public in this fashion (even though she saw the judge in the privacy of his chambers), since we were her own children, and she was a college-educated woman perfectly capable of dealing with finances. Suffragette passion flamed anew—it was because she was a woman these men had made such laws!

On the other hand, the novelty of the important trip excited her, and Mother's day at the courthouse became a big event in the family. She drew on silk stockings, wore a hat, gloves, and touched her cheeks with rouge—she had a date with the law. Certainly there'd been no other men in her life, though she was only thirty-eight when widowed. Later, her account of the interview with the judge made good listening. Judge Bradley's face in photographs appears conventionally Anglo-Saxon handsome, with a direct, virile glance. His public personality was cold, stern, and forbidding; he was deaconlike in bearing. However, his secret home life scandalized the town, for he employed a housekeeper with whom he was also sleeping and who later inherited part of his estate. Salacious tales about his lively bachelorhood abounded, and *that* was why the farmers, angry with him for allowing foreclosures on their farms, put a knife to his private parts.

Mother refused to believe the gossip—such tales were unthinkable, beneath contempt. She respected the judge because he'd reached a station in life of the sort one of us sons might someday get to; in fact, she felt quite comfortable among the elite in any gathering, as if only by a mistaken turn in her life she was not already in such company permanently. If she wondered why Judge Bradley had no wife or children, she would guess it was because of his consuming interest in those tomes lining his chamber walls. He always took more time with her than she'd expected, and discussed other things as well, as if it were a social occasion. But in politics he stayed conservative, while she'd become liberal. She was horrified to hear that a brutal mob had turned upon him merely because his ideas differed from theirs. Violent solutions to social problems seemed barbaric and fruitless. She believed in democracy and shuddered at the mindless *Heils!* coming over the airwaves from Germany. Having studied civic issues, she went to the polls with a purpose, wrote letters to our senators and congressmen, served on juries. Out of chaos, civilization was gradually working toward order and fairness. The assault on Bradley was a momentary plunge into darkness, mere aberration.

For Uncle Jack, the sight of the National Guard troops brought back sweet memories of youth and the Great War. He'd enlisted out of patriotic emotion, but also to rebel from his father, who thoroughly disapproved of such venturing. After all, *his* father's generation had emigrated from Germany after the 1848 upheavals in order to avoid conscription. Furthermore, to think of Germany as the enemy was almost impossible, except for an American son like Jack. These years since the Armistice as a loyal Legionnaire, he felt caretaker of the nation's strength. We always hung out the flag on Memorial Day, Fourth of July, Flag Day, Labor Day, and Armistice Day, though nobody but us and the birds saw the Red, White, and Blue. Now as he glimpsed the khaki-clad troops in puttees and metal-basin hats, with their bivouac tents and transport trucks, he recalled his old buddies, remembered the Doughboys' swift and glorious way of handling trouble. Once again mighty authority, American intervention, would triumph, and these renegade "live wires" of the Holiday would be taught a proper lesson.

"When they're caught, what'll happen to them?" we asked.

"They're in *real* trouble," said Jack.

And so it appeared at first, but eventually only a few went to prison on charges of "assault to commit bodily injury," and the Holiday-elected Democratic governor pardoned them a year later.

"What jail are they putting 'em in?"

"Oh, there're so many prisoners they had to build a bull pen on the country club grounds. I'd sure like to see it. We'll have to drive over and have a look."

"Don't you think of it!" said Lizzie. "Stay clear of *that* trouble! Let's mind our own business."

"But it's something I don't want to miss. And *they* ought to see it too," he said, nodding to the seven of us children in a long row on either side of him at the table. "Never has there been such a thing! All their lives, it's something they'll want to remember."

"Land sakes, I should think we'd want 'em to forget it," said Mother. "At least with Roosevelt in, I feel safer."

We pleaded for a chance to see the bull pen—men herded together into a wire pen intended for bulls. But *no,* Mother corrected (she had a teacher's habit of packing away odd information), the term "bull pen" didn't literally refer to bulls; it was coined in the strike of Colorado mineworkers at the turn of the century. Seizing upon a new argument, we said it would be part of our *education* to see a bull pen, to be a witness of current events of historic importance. It was our *right.*

Our leverage was knowing that the primary aim of family energy was to educate us so well that nothing could stop our dynamic progress in life. We were well aware of Jack's nostalgia over his joyous career of Army freedom at bases around New York City. That was the time of *his* opportunities, a brief moment before circumstances locked him in once more. Each New Year's Day we'd have fresh oysters, which the local grocer imported for us all the way from the Eastern seaboard, packed with shaved ice in cardboard cylinders; and in the basement, in little wooden salt-encrusted kegs, we had a supply of pickled herring, for which he'd gotten a strong taste in Jewish delicatessens. We knew his buddies by the tales he told, and he still felt close to them, though lately none of them wrote letters. Mother, too, had pushed *our* well-being ahead of her own, had subscribed to what social custom deemed suitable for a widow near forty with four children and hadn't tried for a new husband, a new life. She'd considered renewing her teaching certificate and moving to whatever town offered a teaching contract, but felt it would be best for us boys to grow up on the farm with Uncle Jack a substitute father. Having staked so much on our futures, she was upset by these threatening, unexpected events: the Depression, rumors of another world war, and now the outrageous assault on Judge Bradley. She feared being cheated of her prospective enjoyment of seeing us in our successful futures and therefore preferred to ignore violent upheavals such as this. She focused on the rational aspects of life, as if such fidelity to sanity could help keep the world sane.

But Uncle Jack, being an overgrown kid, wanted to see the armored trucks, caissons, and troops—and the Holiday radical farmers in the bull pen. We eagerly went along. The mud road was bumper-to-bumper with sightseers, many of them families of the incarcerated men, hoping to visit or pass messages. "Keep moving, keep moving!" shouted the soldiers on the road. "You can't stop here. Get back in your cars—don't leave 'em on the road. Move!" Sternly militaristic, bayonets fixed to the rifle tips, they strode up and down like a conquering army under the chilly late-April sky. When we'd tried on Jack's ghoulish Army gas mask and steel helmet, this strange equipment of war had seemed improbable, but now before our eyes we saw it authenticated.

The unshaven men in dirty overalls were smiling, laughing, and having a good time behind the stockade wire. On the outside, their friends finger-pointed and gave the prisoners the old horselaugh. Farmers were always herding livestock into pens —now here these guys were, shut up like bulls who had to be kept from the herd. What a good joke! Get out the Kodak, quick. In the carnival, I missed seeing hysterical mothers, if there were any—or worried wives, brothers, fathers—caught only the festive atmosphere of the unusual, exhilaration that now at last *some*thing had been done to shake things up. They talked about J. P. Morgan, on shipboard in mid-Atlantic, who wired to his Wall Street office: WHAT IS HAPPENING IN IOWA. "Even got to old J. P. Morgan himself!"

Jack said that some Holidayers emerged with bloody noses and black eyes from the tent where the military tribunal held its inquiry—smiling over the fact, because he approved of this military roughness. He had a streak of violence in him which sometimes had a terrifying effect upon us. When he razor-stropped the older boys in the washroom for something bad they'd done, he sounded enraged and actually was. In the midst of a temper outburst, he was as blind to reason as a bull seeing red. His example to us meant every grown man reveled now and then in blind, brute strength. He could put aside womanly kindness, gentleness, and dissolve his being in a visceral pool of adrenaline and muscular action. His love of boxing was part of it—every man turned into a fighting stud now and then. In the Army he'd boxed in the ring and was a close follower of the important world championship fights, broadcast on the radio. We'd cluster near him around the Atwater-Kent and listen to the announcer's excited blow-by-blow description. Jack would laugh with ringside blood lust at every powerful thunk and smack. If the bout went fifteen rounds we'd all be exhausted from the intensity of our participation.

He had an athlete's interest in testing his physical skill and muscular strength and measured the worth of any man by it. Like other Jack Armstrong, all-American kids, we came to feel that might made right and to be strong overshadowed considerations of virtue. But since Mother's view was so different, our double vision gave us some distance on this vital question. "It's the *principle* that counts," she'd say.

Any show of power interested Jack: the cyclone that had wrapped a corn elevator around a cottonwood tree; flood waters that had torn out a bridge. The demolished car in last week's head-on was always a wreck he wanted to see. He enjoyed

doing violence to the earth itself (for a good purpose of course)
and terraced the slight hillsides of our land with earth-moving
equipment he'd devised, the pleasure not so much in saving soil
from washing away and having corn plants grow better but in
the great upheaval of dirt. When he lost a finger in a machinery
accident, he took this violence to his person as I expected—with
a shrug and a smile, a nod to the machine's strength.

In every clever triumph of man over rampant Nature, his ego
was enhanced, for in those days it hadn't occurred to anyone
that Nature could ever finally be mastered (and us beaten along
with her). Jack's power mower not only could cut down thriving
weeds before they knew what hit them, he could demolish with
equal ease a five-foot-high snowbank with the whirling blades
of his plow. Nature, the pioneer's awful adversary, was already
staggering, and technology would provide the means to create
finally a man-dominated realm.

To solve his daily farm problems, Jack's brute strength in
the early years was evenly mixed with a reliance upon cunning.
If the Model A slid into a ditch and physics couldn't be employed to get the vehicle out, he could pick up the back end
of the car and lift it up to the road. But as his enormous
muscular power waned, he attended more closely to using his
head, making machines do the work—and thus came closer to
Mother's lifelong emphasis on reason, good sense, and calm
emotions.

As a child, I was sometimes frightened by Jack's insane,
thunderous curses in the machine shed, for I knew no human
being was there to receive them; he was fuming over some
gear not functioning properly, something in the mechanism
misbehaving. Nor could he be kidded into sanity during one
of these blue-streak tirades, for he gave himself over to volcanic
anger as mindlessly as a child having a tantrum. Mother and
Lizzie would shake their heads grimly, disapproving the display,
mindful of the bad example to us. But some feral streak in me
responded to his full-blooded outpouring. I'd seen pictures of
him as a slim, handsome young man on a motorcycle, blasting
around the countryside on the very edge of life-and-death, and

knew that to thrust myself in his direction was halfway desirable. I, too, wished to become lord and master of the universe, nimble, strong, and able to bend the environment to my liking through brute force.

But Mother's way was tantalizing too—safe, somewhat passive, with intellectual justifications for everything. Never mind if they called you a sissy for not fighting: "You showed better sense." But who could believe her? And were A's in arithmetic, spelling, and deportment really preferable to wins on the football field? I was never convinced of that mother-comfort, thanks to our horde of abrasively frank siblings, for we had our own honest eyes and shaped one another according to our vision. And yet each of us threaded his way between these two extremes of direction, at various times taking on one way of life more than the other. We enjoyed being beasts, smelling shotgun powder, killing, destroying—and then we'd turn a tender side and once again feel compassionate to creatures of the world and devoted to intellectual pursuits.

This was no conflict to be settled one way or the other; the two influences threaded their way into my life and became fixed in my personality. In the end it was Mother who resorted to a final violence, who slashed her wrists in an attempt to do away with herself; while my uncle peacefully kept on building his life, making more and more absorbingly interesting machines. His violence had always flown out explosively, consuming itself as he lost his mind in blind anger. While she, increasingly afraid of losing her reason, finally tried that unfamiliar thing—the irrational act.

Mother had hoped to keep from us, in the early years, the information that violence and malignant force existed in the world. We might almost have believed her, were it not for Uncle Jack. He reveled in barbaric strength without guilt, as part of the life he knew and felt; to deny the presence of the irrational, especially in the middle of the twentieth century, would have left us sadly equipped to deal with its incidence. He believed you had to fight to live, be strong or you'd be destroyed, but she cringed from the posture one was thrown into, dealing with such matters. After the attack on Pearl Harbor, each of us boys faced the immediate prospect of violence in its most primitively brutal form; Mother's views on the subject would have only weakened us. Because Jack had so much enjoyed the rough barracks life of the Army, we half-anticipated war adventures for ourselves. It was a pity that the found world turned out to be this way, Mother felt. It *could* all have been different.

After Mother's death in the psychiatric ward of a Sioux City hospital, I learned there'd been a murder in her family which had had a significant role in her story. Aunt Lizzie told me, "I suppose it doesn't make any difference if you know about it now, but your Mother always thought we ought to keep it from you kids."

I was staggered by these grave, preliminary remarks but submitted quietly to her rapt, storyteller's stance, there in the kitchen beside the iron stove, and knew she'd unroll the tale in her own way, for she was a mime, spinner of good anecdotes, quick to catch inflections, able as a mockingbird to imitate anybody's manner, with a tilt of her chin, a lift of her shoulder. We always told her she might have become a great actress.

"Such a thing you try to forget, but just when you think it's far in the past, something comes up to remind you. I probably shouldn't be telling *you*. I never told any of the other kids, but you're the only one who comes around anymore, so I suppose it don't matter."

"Who was it? Who was killed?"

"Uncle Nick shot a man right on the street, in town. No, you never knew Uncle Nick, but you know *who* he is all right . . . Pa's brother . . . your great-uncle." The "relations game" we played on the porch spun in my head quickly. I knew Uncle Nick's grandchildren very well, for these cousins had gone to our one-room country schoolhouse. "Nobody knows all that was behind it, but the man Nick killed was supposed to have been fooling around with Nick's wife."

"But who was he?" I'd never known Lizzie to be so hung

up on her story, unable to get hold of the proper thread to follow.

"You know the Neustaads, do you?"

She was trying to ease the blow, for they were schoolmates in junior high. "It was their grandfather. He had a reputation for being mighty free with the women, both before and after marriage, they said. You know how it is with neighbors in the country—you're in and out of houses, back and forth, all the time. Nobody thinks anything of it—usually. But Nick must've caught Neustaad doing *some*thing, 'cause he said, 'If you ever step foot on my land again, I'll shoot you.'

"After that, they both carried pistols everywhere they went. In saloons, guys would egg them on, saying things to make Uncle Nick jealous and even more suspicious. Then one day on Main Street, they accidentally met on the sidewalk, and Nick shouted something at Neustaad. He whipped out his gun and fired—missing Nick—maybe he shot in the air. The important thing is, he fired the first shot. And Nick fired back, killing him instantly. There were a dozen witnesses." For a moment she said nothing more but looked at my expression on the sly, trying to gauge my reaction.

"What happened to Uncle Nick?" I said coolly.

"The jury was lenient because of the business about the wife . . . that sort of reason is always okay for murder—always justified. And Neustaad fired first."

"He was acquitted then?"

"No, he went to prison for a little while—don't remember just how long. After a year or so he was let out on good behavior. While serving time, he made the nicest little wood carvings of animals for all of us. Don't know *what* happened to ours, but we used to have it in the knickknack cabinet."

"How come none of us knew about any of this?"

"Nobody talked much. It's too small a town, and neighbors have to live with neighbors. Everybody was shocked, but the gossip died away as the years passed. And then . . . a queer thing happened." She paused, turning to look at me with dramatic excitement, for she always saw the story-in-it, the turning that brought the shiver. "Nick's son married and had children, and when the oldest girl grew up, she began dating the oldest Neustaad boy—the grandson of the murdered man, and it was obvious neither of 'em had ever heard about the shooting. Their parents hadn't told 'em.

"It was all hushed up—just like in our family—in order to go on living like nothing terrible had interfered with your life. *That* was like your mother, too, never wanting you kids to know. Time and again you'd ask about Uncle Nick, without realizing the sort of tale you were skirting. She figured if you didn't know bad things in the past, they couldn't hurt you. Well, it doesn't work out that way. And it sure didn't with these two sweethearts. Pretty soon the whole countryside was talking about nothing else. Were they going to marry? Without *knowing*? Shouldn't they be told? Who would?

"Well, somebody did—you can be sure, and I suppose at first they had a hard time believing it. But at last it fell over their romance like a shroud and they decided to break up. She gave him back his diamond. The two families had gotten along okay for a couple generations, just living quietly in the same community, but a marriage would make them relatives—too close altogether—and they weren't going to risk stirring up those old hatreds again. I often wonder how much they really were in love and why they didn't go ahead with the wedding anyhow. After they split up, the boy married a girl who wasn't from around here, but it didn't work out and he was divorced in a year or two. And you know the girl—your cousin, she's married and has a growing family now.

"Makes a person wonder if something like a murder in a family would have to make such a difference. Especially since it happened long ago. But when it came to *us*, I mean when your mother and I were young, going to dances with boy friends, it hadn't happened so awfully long before. As your mother found out."

"Why, what happened?" I felt uneasy by the drift and sensed that all along Lizzie had been wondering how to bring the talk to this point—really, how to prepare *me* for it.

"Well, your mother was awfully sweet on Ben Hames, I guess you knew that. They was goin' steady nearly a year, and he seemed as serious about her as she was about him. I used to tag along like kid sisters do, when they went skating. I'd hold the lantern for 'em. And I can tell you, they made an awful good-looking couple. I thought sure they was going to marry. Carrie had been teaching about ten years and some folks thought she'd waited too long, that she might have trouble catching a man, though she was awfully pretty and had won a beauty contest at Mapleton, where she taught. The only thing about Ben—he was terribly religious, and *our* family didn't belong to any church at all. Pa was pretty lax about those things. Of course, Carrie never imagined religion would interfere with her romance. She figured she'd take an adult confirmation class and join the Lutheran church. I mean, she wasn't a *Catholic,* or anything. But Ben acted very peculiar about the whole issue. He said he didn't know how he could marry her because she didn't belong to any church at all—his family would never approve. It was such a shock to Carrie—that he'd *say* a thing like that! She really couldn't believe it. 'But tell your Pa I'm willing to *join* the Lutheran church,' she said. Ben only shook his head, saying it wouldn't do any good, with his folks, because of—'because of the other thing that happened.' '*What* other thing?' she asked. And then Ben said, 'Your Uncle Nick killed a man.'"

"So they broke up—over that?"

"Carrie was so mad at him she said she'd never go out with him again. Humiliated, too—to have it thrown in her face that way, something she couldn't help in the least."

We walked into the living room because Lizzie wanted me to see the photograph of Nick's widow, which we had among the other family portraits on the piano. "She's still living—eighty-three! And Neustaad's been dead for sixty years—just think of it!"

I did, looking at the wrinkled, leathery face, skimpy white hair, small, alert eyes—and tried to imagine the fierce passion she'd aroused. "Your mother started dating your dad not long after the breakup with Ben, and she married him pretty fast. So that's how come Henry was your father, not Ben."

That's what violence did to my life, even before I existed. "That's what a killing can do," I said. And then we left each other, as if something holy had happened between us.

10. Next of Kin

The third Sunday in June we'd leave the farm early in the morning for the two-hundred-mile trip "back East" to the Greiman family reunion—Grandmother's people, though she herself, being too frail, never went. The original nine Greiman siblings dwindled until (when Grandma passed ninety) we were representatives of the last living pioneer Greiman. Each of those nine brothers and sisters spawned families who produced children, who generally married young. Their extensive acreages in the vicinity of Mason City lay side by side, whole sections of rich land, like a principality.

With their days lived in isolation, farmers often failed to develop ways of opening themselves to others; how convenient, therefore, to feel an immediate closeness with a cousin because you shared a common ancestor. At funerals the entire church might be filled with mourners who were kin. Physical proximity quickly warmed into a nourishing companionship. With such an army to deploy against death, who wouldn't feel heartened? Our numerous parthenogenetic selves couldn't be vanquished; there were always more bodies to pour into the maw of life.

We traveled farthest to these reunions because Grandma had gone away the greatest distance, married to her homesteading, pioneer husband. Perhaps because two girl-children of this union, Bertha and Elizabeth, never married, a lifelong closeness to the eastern Iowa cousins remained very important. My aunts maintained an emotional attachment to their female cousins that continually astonished us. We never felt anything when we were pushed toward our third and fourth cousins, children we'd never seen before, and urged to become acquainted for life. We could never remember these kids' names from one year to the next. But in the early days when young ladies like Bertha and Elizabeth were restricted in their coursings through the world, visits to cousins took on all the importance of an excursion— and worried parents *had* to allow these trips. Breath of the larger world wafted over them on their pilgrimages from home to home; in traveling one stayed with relatives, lest one insult them by putting up at a hotel. When Jack and Lizzie married, they toured the Greiman cousins on their honeymoon, a trial no doubt for Lizzie—on display as a bride, to be judged, criticized. They proceeded from farm to farm, staying a few days, moving on, until Lizzie had met the whole clan. She was impressed by such a mass solidarity of kinship, having sprung from a straggly bunch of people who kept losing each other, going off and never coming back, never writing, even.

On these June Sundays the Greiman reunion took over an entire state park picnic ground. Each family brought a pot-luck contribution: an abundant spread resulted, far beyond our considerable stomach capacities. Picnic tables were pushed together, laid with cloths, and the food extended from one end to the other, as if some Jesus thought he had to feed five thousand. Actually, there were often well over two hundred Greimans, and what squeals of joy among the middle-aged! Embraces, hugs, and tears of family happiness. The sheer excitement over the continuing narrative of their lives transported them. The day would be spent informing themselves of all that had taken place since the last meeting: what new babies had been born, who was dying, what each child was doing, who had married—the same old human news but in an annual fresh arrangement that seemed enthralling. We were always pleased to hear that big fat Cousin Bill from Blue Earth, Minnesota, had arrived as usual with several huge cylinders of ice cream packed in dry ice, for he was in the ice-cream business. Every worthy family needed one such member.

How strange, to spend the Sunday among all those hearty strangers who knew your name and sometimes grabbed you and squeezed hard, recognizing the father in you, or their "Aunt Liza" or "Aunt Louisa" (Grandmother), whom they hadn't seen for a couple of decades. The family was a great banyan tree of human life, limbs everywhere, all of them part of you, and you sometimes pined for the day when nobody would know who you were or press with a blood claim. The cities in recent decades have filled with escapees from the nearness of flesh. And yet I liked it—this serene ignoring of my special self, plus the aura of self-congratulation in the simple fact that we all belonged to the same tribe. The truth was, this Greiman clan wasn't so special. All over Iowa throughout the summer other family reunions took place, and in Long Beach, California, an annual gigantic Iowa picnic was held, reminiscent of the real thing—which we were having here. We celebrated the very gift of life, honored our ancestors, and paid homage to the extraordinary fact that we existed on earth simultaneously, in this moment of time, with fibers of the same chromosomes threading our beings.

Well-trained children were expected to give comfort and pleasure to their elders, and our role in the Greiman reunion was to provide entertainment on "the program" after the picnic. Each branch of the family contributed one number: a dramatic reading, Chautauqua style; a song; or a piece played on some instrument. Since we were the only children of our branch, one of us had to perform—partly so that when we were up there on the platform under the white oaks, everybody could have a good look at our Greimanish high cheekbones and solid body frames. One year I played "The Bells of St. Mary's" on my clarinet, the reed going dry in my nervous mouth, squeaking sounds from the tube. At other reunions, Brother Ken played his cornet, Ruth played Schubert on the piano (in a church hall, a Sunday it rained), and Cousin Lois rendered a solo on her flute.

The war and gas rationing canceled the Greiman reunions, and, once interrupted, they never got going again. The first-cousin Greimans were only reunited at funerals, when some of their own generation began to drop away from life—surprising them because of their still youthful feelings inside, which bore no resemblance to the sagging look of their bodies and wrinkled skins. Their cousin-closeness had arisen as a conspiracy of children united in a special way. Their old-fashioned, pioneer parents, uncles, and aunts had seemed well ahead of them in years; now suddenly here they found themselves in the vanguard, approaching the dark edge on the rim of oblivion. Suddenly they were old, and they had no more joyous June reunions. Even their grandchildren were mature enough to marry and produce children, in the rural two-decades-to-a-generation way. The great Greiman family had spread so wide it was disappearing into the universal family and no longer could be identified.

Mother and Lizzie were not to be outdone by this array of patrilineal ancestry. *They* had a few of their own, and we children must be reminded we were only half German—Danish through our maternal grandmother, Swiss through our maternal grandfather. Our mongrelism provided relief from too much Teutonic blood-consciousness, and yet Mother had a difficult time making our lineage clear to us. She knew every branch of the tree and could trace family connections when asked, but since her real mother had died before the twentieth century began, it was hard for me to feel any ancestral bond. All we had by which to remember this grandmother was a shoe box full of sepia photographs of unnamed Danish country people, focused but faded, all of them with the slanty Lapp eyes I inherited and which gave a somewhat Oriental look to each of us (enabling me, when living in Iran, to pass for a Kurdish tribesman). Her father, Grandpa Rudolph, had died before I was born, too, leaving his widow, their stepmother, whom I was definitely not to confuse with a genuine relative.

One summer afternoon, Mother drove us all to a distant, hilly part of the county to meet an uncle she hadn't seen for years, because "I want you kids to know him." Whether he was her true mother's brother or kin of one of those other mothers she had (her father married three times) wasn't clear, but we'd long noted that Mother's people didn't make as much of relatives as the paternal side did. On the journey we were thrilled by the sudden plunges over steep hills, which dropped the bottoms out of our stomachs, but Mother was unhappy traversing such poor land and deduced from the scenery that her uncle wasn't doing well. The dirt thoroughfare we traveled was called the Broken Kettle Road, one of the few named routes in the region. We were enthralled by the appropriateness of the title. The farm was as poor-looking as expected, with a couple of scraggly willows set near unpainted barns. We tumbled out of the plush car seats bursting with eagerness to meet a new sugar uncle, for every one of these species met thus far had turned out to be a smiling, gift-bearing man who delighted in the role his relationship cast him in. Our disappointment was sharp, then, to find a slack-faced, woebegone man who could scarcely muster a flicker of interest toward us and made no effort to remember our names or inquire our ages. Nor did he possess any offspring cousins for us to play with; no ample-bosomed aunt came from the kitchen bearing a plate of cookies and a lemonade pitcher. This uncle had no idea what was expected of him, and he couldn't imagine why Mother had insisted on paying him a visit. Old times didn't interest him, and he had trouble recalling just what his family connection truly was. We packed ourselves back into the car and left without even entering the house. Mother did not voice her disappointment but on the way home drove especially fast over those steep hills of the Broken Kettle Road, our stomachs falling. Memory of the visit which had come to nothing quickly dropped away.

This dismal day of family coldness was typical of Mother's

people. They were so often unwilling or unable to make the
crucial blood recognitions. A history of kinship failures stretched
back to her father, Rudolph, born in 1853, son of a Bern
harnessmaker—*he* nearly lost himself at the age of three, when
he strayed from his parents in Paris, while they were en route
to America. He was missing so long his father and mother
(having sunk all their savings in the passage tickets) almost
gave up the search and left for their ship—in which case we
might all have been French, we mused, delighted by the notion.
The mystery of lost identities was the intriguing opposite of
knowing all too clearly exactly how you were placed in a kinship.

My grandfathers homesteaded in Iowa only four and a half
miles from each other, both of them coming west with the railroad. But while one grandfather's fortune flourished and his line
took root and flowered, the other's didn't. Mother's father had
bad luck with his wives: they kept dying on him. The first
wife, parent of mother's half sister Rose and half brother John,
expired one year after arrival on the homestead. The next marriage, in 1888, was to my Danish grandmother; she produced
three children before she died ten years later. Finally, Grandfather Rudolph took up with a handsome widow of a saloon-
keeper, who already had five children, and although she became
crippled and was confined to a wheelchair, she outlived him.

With such peculiar shoots and suckers on the pruned family
tree, coherence was difficult to pass on to our generation. Notions of blood pride with these relatives kept getting obscured by
feelings of closeness toward children of Mother's stepsisters and
stepbrothers, who were no actual relation at all. Some of these
kids boarded with us during the years we drove eleven miles to the
high school in the county seat town; they became dearer to us
than any of our real cousins, children of mother's brother Frank
—who were Catholics and whom we saw only occasionally.

Uncle John, Mother's half brother, caught the message of
kinship but failed to hold himself responsible for making his
contribution. He thought just being a relative was all you had
to do. He'd arrive from Godforsaken places to see us now and
then, for family funerals, and he fit right in because he had the

characteristic look of Mother's people: the soulful eyes, dark hair, and brooding, distant manner, which disappeared at the hint of surface humor into a wide smile and white teeth. He bore the lacerations of life with a sheepish, bewildered look, yet continued to offer his sweet disposition in the world, eschewing bitterness, though he'd been slapped down at every turn. Mother and Lizzie always made much of their half brother John, on his infrequent appearances, and he responded to this kinship warmth with a touching eagerness. He too believed blood was thicker than water.

Grandfather Rudolph had once hoped that John, his first-born son, would take over the homestead and continue the heritage, as happened in other pioneer families, but John loved to play the violin and fiddled for a fee at local dance halls, then received engagements farther and farther away, as if his own music were Pied Pipering him and nobody, not even a father, could disenchant him. John met his wife, Inez, while playing a roadhouse job in Minnesota, and they were married in 1914. As soon as the romance was legally sealed, Inez demanded he stay home and not travel, and so he had to give up fiddle-playing. Since farming was the only other thing he knew how to do, he rented land in Flandreau, South Dakota, for a couple of years, until he'd accumulated sufficient stake to buy a homestead in the new country north of Fargo. There, on the flat open prairie he tried to become a wheat farmer and cattle rancher. Roads had not yet been graded into civilized square patterns, and in winter snow drifted into the deep coolies that eroded the tableland. If your car fell in you'd freeze to death.

Lizzie, Jack, and Aunt Bertha packed up a tent and out-door cooking equipment and took a camping trip to Buffalo, North Dakota, to see how John was doing—the summer of 1923. When they finally found their way and approached the farm-stead, white turkeys were roosting on the hayrack and from a distance Lizzie thought Inez had her washing out. The barn was only a wooden frame with straw blown over it, where animals could find some shelter in winter. The house was a mere one-room cabin, and there on canvas cots the guests from Iowa slept, while Inez wept hysterically half the night in a dark corner. John privately told them next day that, after the birth of her daughter Frances, Inez had "never been quite right." She had "really bad spells" because "the life out here is too hard for her."

A few months later he committed her to a state insane asylum, and in order to be in town for every allowable visiting day, he attended barbering school and learned the trade, set up shop. But after several years his hands began to tremble so violently "from an allergy to hair" that he was unable to barber. He lived meagerly on the income from his ranch, which was now successfully rented, and in time became acquainted with an agreeable high school English teacher, whom he planned to marry someday. But he wouldn't think of hurting Inez, and state laws made divorce a long court procedure, considering her circumstances. John and his friend kept company but never lived together, perhaps never slept together. By the time Inez died, the teacher was so close to her minimum pension year she kept working after marrying John—but keeled over with a heart attack and died. John decided to return to his ranch as a sort of punishment, perhaps, or to ferret out the curse of his luck, confronting it head-on, in the lair of despondency which he knew best. His daughter Frances was married and gone—he had no one. For years we lost him entirely. Mother and Lizzie received no word even at Christmas; letters were returned stamped Address Unknown.

At age sixty-three he unexpectedly showed up "for a home visit," and his sisters joyously installed him in an upstairs bedroom quickly vacated by one of us. John seemed vague, bemused, a little wandering in the head. On the train trip he'd lost a suitcase, but he didn't know how—or where to begin the baggage trace. By now it was clear he'd inherited the bad luck curse of his father: he attached himself to women who died on him. He'd married again recently, only to experience the same thing. He and his late wife had worked the Yellowstone Park motels and cabins in summer. "A nice vacation for us," he said with a smile, but we never found out what they were having a

vacation *from*. His only child Frances now had five offspring—
"she produced pretty good," he said, farmerishly, but he'd not
seen his grandchildren in many years, for Frances and her family
traveled around the country in a trailer, working carnivals. Her
first husband, an older man, had constructed a clever mechanical logging-camp display, for which they charged admission;
and after he died, Frances and her new carnie-husband continued with the attraction. "They always like to set up near the
church booth," said John, as if this preferred location indicated a spiritual wholesomeness, and not that church bingo-
booths drew large crowds.

For several days John lounged around the house, visiting with
his sisters every chance he could catch them, between jobs. I
wondered about the hurt, vulnerable look in his eyes. Something about our teeming, thriving household almost moved him
to tears. We'd catch him staring at us with a Godlike love, un-
reachable and terrifying. We knew John was a good man who
must somehow keep his faith in life. He had a clean, antiseptic
smell, a bachelor's dryness devoid of the juices of humanity,
which kept all of us limber and lubricated, exuding odors of life.

Our household welcome was warm, unquestioning, automatic,
but clearly he wasn't used to such open, affectionate generosity.
He'd not been around a family for so long. Lizzie and Mother
deftly set about building a nest of relationships for him to cozy
into: John was to stay here with us but spend his days visiting
other relatives. By renewing family bonds he'd long ago let fade,
John sought to heal himself. He'd ask earnestly about the various
cousins, and Lizzie would reply, "Oh *yes,* you must see him—
he'd be terribly disappointed if you didn't." And we listened to
these lies knowing why they were said; but John believed them.

A favorite cousin, Walter, had moved away only last year.
"To Vermilion, South Dakota?" John asked. "Why in the world
did he go there?"

"You see, his oldest girl was ready to enter college, and they
figured it would be cheaper to move to a college town than send
her off and pay room-and-board bills. Nothing to hold them
here, anyhow, when you come down to it," said his sister, Lizzie.

All he did was watch over his farms and do a little landlord repairing now and then. He'd lived off his inheritance most of his life and didn't have to work.

A few relatives had died, events John hadn't heard of, and these shocks unsettled his growing well-being. *"No!* Dead? How could that be? He's younger than *I* am!" When he showed signs of sinking into moroseness, Lizzie countered with vigorous optimism: "There're so *many* folks who can't wait to see you—they'll be tickled pink! First of all you'd better go to town and find Brother Frank. He's right there in his new retirement house and easy to find—or else downtown playing cards with the other old farmers. It'll be so good for him—seeing you. Give him something new to think about."

Uncle Frank had lately been undergoing severe trials of adjustment to his life of leisure, after the heavy routines of the country. His face had become puffily white, his arthritic legs had gotten worse and he could scarcely walk; added to these real ailments with a growing streak of hypochondria. This fiery, jokester uncle, full of beans, bursting with fun, now felt there was nothing ahead of him but death, and he couldn't enjoy the supposed pleasures of not having to work. Card-playing at the Farmer's Tap provided a few hours of daily forgetfulness, and he'd even taken up fancywork to fill his hours, excusing himself from the smoke-fogged saloon by saying in a falsetto, "Sorry, boys, deal me out—I've got to get home and tend to my knitting."

In his gleaming new home, Uncle Frank welcomed his half brother and enjoyed showing John the modern, convenient arrangements—tangible rewards for those years of farm labor. Then they settled down in the living room in front of the TV set, a great novelty. Uncle Frank's attention kept wandering toward the screen; finally they stopped talking altogether and watched the programs come on, one soap opera after another. At last John rose and said he'd like to visit Cousin Albert—would Frank drive him out to the farm, if he still lived there? Well, yes, Albert remained in the country, but since he'd recently undergone surgery he probably couldn't have a visitor for long—

better phone, first. They made the journey, but Frank remained behind the wheel of his car while John went into the house, for he figured it'd be a short visit and he felt extremely nervous about getting mired down in the mud.

At the end of the day, when Lizzie heard from John about the abortive visits, she shook her head in dismay. "But you and Albert were the *best* of friends. You'd have *so* much to talk over! You'll just have to go back and have a *really* good long talk. One of the boys will drive you." But John's narwhale-wrinkled brow and painful expression revealed he'd prefer not to. Albert and he had exhumed as much of their past relationship as either of them could find—no point in returning for more dredging. Next day Uncle Frank drove John to a stepsister's house in town and said to him, "Come on down to the Tap when you're through, and have a game of cards with the gang." The stepsister was dead and John didn't know what to talk to her husband about, since he'd never known him well. They compared notes on what their children were up to these days, and ran out of further things to say.

Nothing could save Uncle John from a knowledge relentlessly pressing in upon him: in his long absence since 1914, everyone had forgotten him. Nobody was interested in what had happened to him during these intervening years, not even his blood relatives. Only Lizzie and Mother insisted on making real a connection that had once held, long ago in their youthful past; he was truly their half brother and they loved him, were concerned for his welfare. They sensed that John had held this world, which he'd left behind in time and distance, as some sort of reserve measuring place where he could sum up meanings, take account of things, and particularly: where he'd always feel most at home because this region *was* his birthplace and these were his people. If one scratches the surface of nostalgia, a certain itch is pleasurably assuaged, but there's a limit to how much of this one can take; John's cousins felt no honest bond with him at all.

Now that his visit was fizzling, Lizzie thought of a new plan for John to continue his pursuit of the dream. She urged him to travel to Bakersfield, California, to see his sister Rose, whom he'd not glimpsed in forty years. "You never know, something might happen and you'd never get to see her." I felt Lizzie was veering dangerously close to the unmentionable lurking behind all this activity on Uncle John's part. He was floundering in a dark knowledge held just a little bit away: everything for him had suddenly become a matter of life-and-death. It seemed to me that this brother and sister hadn't cared much about each other or they'd have made some effort to visit, these many years. As the penitent turns to God in the last minutes in order to be saved, Uncle John clung to the ladders of relationship—for here in the labyrinth of family he'd find some meaning to his life. Yes, he resolved to go visit Sister Rose. For Lizzie it was important that her brother undertake the family rituals which he'd so long denied himself. Tracing an outward form sometimes brought inner meanings into being. Creator and the created were flanks of the same vestigial thing. She also wanted to see him round out his life, almost as in a drama; since his family stage had been bare so long, now was the time for a grand-entrance gesture. He was heartened by her urgings, by her wholehearted faith that life could be patterned, formed, and that *he* was the actor—that now was the time for him to step forth.

He exited from our lives.

Years later when Uncle John died (he'd since returned to the Dakotas), his two sisters had preceded him, but Jack, living alone in the farmhouse, decided to fulfill the family promises to that man: he would attend the funeral, just as Lizzie and Carrie would have wanted. He climbed into his car and headed north to Anita, North Dakota, lost his way and drove fifty miles off the route, and didn't arrive in the tiny village until nine-thirty at night, when the only restaurant was about to close. He over-heard the waitress talking to the cook about "getting the church cleaned up good, for tomorrow," and revealed his identity—that he'd traveled all this distance for his brother-in-law's funeral. They were dumfounded to hear this news, heartened but also astonished to learn once again that family members could care deeply for one another. Jack's appearance helped them keep faith. Frances and her carnival-worker husband were the only other relatives for the event, and the three mourners slept upstairs in John's house that night. The chief thing troubling the dry-eyed daughter was that, since her father's body was lying in a funeral home twenty miles away, she hadn't been able to check whether or not the grave had been dug. Jack promised to drive over in the morning to see about it.

The undertaker, cheerful and efficient, said everything was in order; "this is the first one—this season"—he'd kept nine bodies in cold storage through the winter, the ground being too frozen to chip into. A small but intent group of people gathered in church for the funeral service. Afterwards, Frances dealt with the real estate agent into whose hands she placed disposition of the house. The furniture was donated to a church benefit and missionaries got the clothes, for overseas heathens. Frances kept only two boxes of photograph albums and other personal items, which easily fit into the car trunk. Next morning she and her husband stepped into their vehicle with its Arkansas license plates, and Jack got into his, with Iowa plates—and they left North Dakota.

This relentlessly exposed ending to Uncle John's life was exactly what he'd sensed years earlier; it lurked behind the strange, haunted look in his eyes. He knew all along the bleak terms of existence but kept hoping his sisters and other relatives would keep that knowledge a little away from him. Why does everyone know the sadness of life yet insist upon finding some other answer? Lizzie and Mother did their best and pushed forward the comforting news a family is capable of imparting: see, there's enough love for everyone, and here are all these human beings, flesh of your flesh, stirring with life. *For God so loved the world* . . . Now come away, from your hole of loneliness.

But I know, in hard rural life nothing clutters the directness of one's insight regarding these matters; no illusions obtain if a wrenching, true reality pierces one's very soul. The result might be a sorrow so deep nothing further need be discovered in any direction. Few can bear to live hugging such a bone-grinding vision, and so we in our family lifted our eyes and dreamt of paradise someday in California or burrowed into the myths of family, swaddled by our kinship, warmed by the blood of our blood. As long as the strands of relationship held, the world was not so cold.

11. *These Mothers*

Father's three sisters were childless and looked upon us as their family; with Lizzie and Carrie that made five mothers altogether. In 1918, Aunt Anne accompanied Lizzie when she traveled east to Jamaica, Long Island, to visit her fiancé, Jack, who was stationed at Camp Mills, and there Anne met Ernest, fell in love, and married soon after the Armistice. Father loaned Ernest and Anne a thousand dollars to start them farming, in Minnesota, but the venture failed along with the marriage and Anne did penance for her mistake by working as a short-order cook and waitress in a railroad restaurant. The small, southern Minnesota switching town was safely removed from the home scene, and the truth about her grass-widowhood might never be known. Only wicked, ungodly people were divorced; she'd made her marital bed and would hence lie on it. Decades passed but she never told her mother that her husband wasn't living with her, yet Grandma knew. When Christmas gift tags were inscribed to us "Uncle Ernest" as well as "Aunt Anne," we caught the fakery but also understood her pride and, without having to be told to keep mum, bolstered her up by pretending to believe the lie.

For years Ernest hovered on the edges of our life like a

wizened, unpredictable wolf: tall, rangy, gray-haired, grinning, with a whiny voice and pockets full of Dentyne chewing gum. He'd show up now and then, hoping to get a foothold among us, but we gave him short shrift; once the dismissal was so abrupt Ernest drove to the neighbors' and slept the night there, paying for his keep by telling sly tales of his mistreatment. At sixty-five, Aunt Anne retired on Social Security and came home to live with Grandma, the marriage mess still never discussed between them. When Grandma died, Ernest pounced at once. In secret whereabouts a hundred miles away, he heard the news (who phoned him, we wondered?) and arrived in time for the funeral, to walk soberly down the aisle with his wife, Anne, to the mourner's pew, where he proceeded to weep his silly head off, sobbing all through the service. We were determined he'd not get a penny of the family money. Uncle Jack, drawing upon old Army days, persuaded him to sign quit-claim papers so that he'd never fall heir to a portion of the farm. Ernest did outlive Anne, but avariciousness was weak in him by this time and what little estate she possessed had been safely consigned to her surviving sister, and he didn't try to contest it.

When Uncle Jack lived alone in the big farmhouse, Ernest saw his chance to move in, live cozy under a comfortable eave, be looked after. "But I wouldn't have that good-for-nothing bum on *my* hands! Sure, *he'd* like nothing better! But I told him to get moving." Ernest's casual catch-jobs had included taking care of a town ball park, janitor in a school, and work as an orderly in a state mental hospital—or perhaps he was a patient there. We heard rumors he'd been arrested for molesting children and may have done time in prison. When he was dying, finally, in the Veterans Hospital in Sioux Falls, South Dakota, Jack drove up to visit him, for the hospital social worker wrote to him as "nearest kin." Curious, won by the story-in-it, Jack *had* to see the tale of Ernest through to the very end, since he was the only one left at home to do it. I'd have done the same—for the old fool.

Whatever hell Ernest caused Aunt Anne, she refused to soil the home nest with it, for a thing unacknowledged did not exist;

in the warm glow of our farm life, the reality of seedy Ernest faded. We sensed in her a great need for love, the reflex from anguish making the need deeper than in our two other aunts, for they remained maidens who'd kept themselves free of emotional scourgings, perhaps wisely. We'd rush our sugarplum selves toward Aunt Anne to assuage her pain, to fill out her love grief.

The year I was nine, her birthday present to me was oddly enough a new striped overall. She pretended to urge my acceptance of this utilitarian gift by praising the sturdy goods. What a nice overall indeed it was! To which I grudgingly responded by following her insistence that I inspect it very carefully. I was sinking inside over this lost opportunity to receive something really interesting for a present, since it was rare to have Aunt Anne home for my birthday at all. And so, out of the depths of my disappointment, I suddenly came upon a set of colored jacks, deep in a side pocket, a pearl-handled knife in another, a compass in another. Feverishly I examined all six pockets and each of them contained a treasure. How she laughed!

At Christmas when she traveled from Minnesota, she never arrived in time to view our performances in the Christmas Eve church pageant—but next morning, on an early train, and she didn't have to pay fare because the trainmen loved her. Not only did her terrible Scrooge boss force her to work Christmas Eve, but he and his horrid wife paid her so little trainmen kept slipping her big tips to help out. After Christmas Day church services, we'd have the banquet at the farm, served on our best white linen tablecloth with the silver and crystal that had been wedding presents to the two mothers of the house. Aunt Anne would take a nap, and when she awoke we'd begin our present-opening. Elizabeth, the teacher from Detroit, gave us the latest Parker games and expensive gifts from Hudson's department store. Bertha, who owned the hat shop, knew our Santa Claus lists and what hadn't been under the tree for our early morning discovery. Anne's limited funds meant modest presents which out of politeness we weren't to compare with the grander bounty from her sisters.

All three of these protomothers needed the farm for their nourishment. Even in far-off Detroit, Elizabeth received eggs by mail in little metal cartons. She enjoyed a glamorous city life of concerts, theater, golf-playing, bridge-party socials, and trips with girl friends to national parks, but she always nestled back into Iowa during her two-month vacation in summer, staying in Grandpa's town house with her sister Bertha and Grandma —hanging onto her girlhood that way. Aunt Anne had lost her childhood forever because of that errant husband; now her only pleasure was to look at us in ours—and her large brown eyes behind glasses would fill with tears. She'd wipe her wet cheeks (we'd pretend not to notice) with a tiny, fancily embroidered handkerchief. We'd try to ease the sorrow of her life by kissing her a lot, to which she'd respond with such strong bear hugs she almost squeezed the breath out of us. Even her excessive weight —arms like loaves of dough—seemed to bear upon the heaviness of her life and drag her down. She suffered from edema and wrapped her swollen legs in elastic bandages. We'd look at her wounded limbs and think of all those hours she stood in the restaurant, feeding people between trains. Her cooking arts were wasted on those transients, who only wanted ham and eggs and a piece of apple pie. When Aunt Anne died after happy years of retirement living with her sister, it came suddenly, while pulling on her stockings. A blood clot reached her heart. "Oh dear, I think I'm going," she said to Elizabeth. *"Lord,* here I come!"

While the three aunts felt as much at home on the farm as we did (for they'd grown up here), the same couldn't be said for Lizzie, who was always trying to prove herself, continually uncertain she was worthy enough to be settled here. Marrying into this family had been her sister Carrie's idea first. In those close-blooded days, the first decades of this century, family members helped each other find spouses. Romance between Lizzie and Jack blossomed after my parents married. Lizzie and Mother's people had neither money, land, nor "reputation," and so these marriages seemed to be a step up for the girls. Father's family had a smugness about them; any newcomers to the fold, they felt, should feel mightily set up by the honor. However, Mother had no craven attitude toward her husband's folks, since education gave her self-confidence. What were they after all but a bunch of farmers who still clung strongly to old German ways?

Aunts Bertha and Elizabeth were regular summer-night visitors, usually at dusk, after they'd finished their many home and garden projects, arriving like visiting fairy godmothers, in the shiniest, newest Ford on the market. They brought with them news of goings-on in town, the fresh scent of good perfume, and a special, doting interest in each child. We wallowed in their attention, climbing over their ample laps, kissing and fondling them, much to their delight—with an abandon we didn't exhibit for our true mothers—we'd have been ridiculed for such behavior by our siblings. The aunts came to pick produce from our field garden, which had been extensively planted in anticipation of such foraging. Or there were mulberries, raspberries, strawberries to harvest; from girlhood times, they knew all the trees and bramble lanes and wandered freely, pans in hand. Meanwhile, Jack slipped a basket of two dozen clean white eggs into their car, and later we'd all sit on the front porch until it grew "cool enough to sleep," and talk was good.

For Lizzie these visits sometimes seemed inspections. Should one of the aunts reach down to pull a stray weed, she was insulted. If they offered to help with the supper dishes, perhaps it was a criticism that the job hadn't been done yet. She feared the housekeeping might not seem up to the gleaming family standard when these "girls" had lived here. She tried her best to make her food as tasty as anything her sisters-in-law could produce. We children must be as well behaved as little automatons, particularly in church. (Although a late communicant in the Lutheran fold, she'd show she could be as pious as anyone.) "How're the crops coming along?" to Brother Jack from his sister, Bertha, might mean, Lizzie felt: *We're the landlords over part of this farm and how well are you working our acres?* My paternal grandfather's estate remained unsettled for years. Jack paid cash rent to his sisters in the name of his mother, although it wasn't clear how much was owed and to whom—this place was in every sense the family farm. Lizzie bridled under the sloppy arrangement, feeling Jack was being taken advantage of by everyone; and yet she knew nothing would be done about it. And *she* was the newcomer.

In order for the joint project of child-rearing to succeed, the two mothers had to suppress jealousies and minor irritations; with so much physical labor expected of them, they had no stamina or time left for spatting. We seven children were up there on the altar of their lives, *that's* all that mattered. Consequently, throughout these years I saw the sisters in equable, side-by-side co-operation. One of them couldn't be played off against the other—by any of us—for along with Uncle Jack, they were like the Trinity, inseparable in parenthood.

Each woman's talent was given its due: Mother was house-keeper, Lizzie cook and laundress. While Mother could prepare a meal if she had to (and did Monday washdays), we laughed how often the toast burned, for she'd be discussing politics and forget the stove. Lizzie prepared delicious pork roasts with herbs, baked sour cherry pies, cinnamon coffeecakes, bread. She cannily noted what dish struck our palates most strongly, and managed to have it served a fair number of times; she knew the cupboard-hold she had on us. Mother attended to dishwashing, ironing, house-cleaning, with a staff of children assigned to wield mops and cloths. The whir of Mother's bedroom sewing machine filled the afternoon hours; she'd darn socks, patch holes, mend rips. She taught the two girl-children how to embroider, crochet, and make dresses from paper patterns. She also gave us haircuts, Saturday afternoons; one by one we climbed on top of the kitchen stool and submitted our heads to her pinching clippers. During the severe winter of 1936, she directed the family—even Uncle Jack—in a cottage-industry venture: we wove an enormous orange and brown afghan, each of us working on little nail-toothed square looms, weaving the yarn in and out. Mother pieced the great cover together in its proper arrangement of squares. Sewing was her personalized gift of love to us, just as cooking was Lizzie's, and she was aware of the intimacy of this needle power. When I left home for college and the life of a scholar, to sit long hours on a hard chair at my desk, she presented me with a small, tufted cushion of her own making; and when I married, her wedding present was a couple of elaborately embroidered pillow slips upon which to lay our heads.

In the cat population that swirled around the house, I dubbed one female "the Lizzie-cat," for she and her sister were both mothers. Smiling wryly over the analogy, Lizzie saw further parallels, for the Lizzie-cat was rather jumpy and anxious, her cheekbones stood out prominently, and the whole face with its short nose and high forehead caught a certain Lizzie-resemblance. That cat could never be completely convinced she belonged on the south porch along with every other cat.

Lizzie deferred to her sister's judgment on important family decisions because she was younger and hadn't been educated beyond the eighth grade. And yet on the scale of life's advantages, *she* had the living husband. Jack's muscles and force kept us moving. Mother might decide we children should travel by car eleven miles to the county seat town, bypassing the ill-equipped local high school, but it was Uncle Jack who produced the Model A Ford, kept it running properly, and engineered the working out of the scheme. And thus an equilibrium held.

The mission of these mothers was to make it possible for us to have different, better lives than theirs. No one felt this more keenly than Lizzie, whose high intelligence informed her that her numerous talents hadn't been developed, that she'd "missed out." Although she loved school, being the youngest she was the child to stay home when her stepmother became ill—her arm had "swelled to the size of a crock," and she pleaded for Lizzie's help. "How the little one can run!" she told her husband, Rudolph, speaking from her helpless immobility in a wheelchair. Lizzie contributed her services because her father also asked it of her. Foolishly, he'd married the handsome widow with five children because he thought his own motherless offspring needed maternal attention, giving no credence to the truth of fairy tale legends on the natural ways of stepmothers. Nor did he

understand the openness of childhood savagery and how pref-
erences of treatment are cunningly sought.

Occasionally Lizzie told us of those early years under the stepmother's reign—of a March 1 moving day, when the family left
the homestead, all their goods packed in grain wagons. The
stepmother had been used to the comforts of city life, not *this!*
Lizzie heard the other children lamenting over their discovery
that they'd forgotten a pet cat, left him behind. She volunteered
to ride horseback and return to the farm, although the wagons
were already a mile down the road. Her father tried to stop her
but she insisted, leapt upon a horse, and set off barebacked, her
legs clinging to the horse's flanks. Then she wandered all over
the empty farm, calling the cat's name, hearing only echoes of
her forlorn cry. The deserted place frightened her, particularly
the shriveled-in-size rooms of the deserted house. When she
finally found the cat in the basement, he seemed a stray like herself. Weeping, she clutched him to her breast. But in those few
hours of having been left behind (or reacting to her fierce
embrace), the cat went wild, clawing her. She hung onto him
and mounted the horse. When she caught up with the wagons,
her father shouted *Lizzie, Lizzie, what's happened?* for her
arms were raw, her face scratched and bleeding. The cat she'd
been holding so tightly dropped dead upon the road. The boys
kicked it angrily into the ditch. Now the proud stepmother on
the high seat for once paid no attention to her own children but
lavished concern upon little Lizzie, taking her into her arms,
comforting her. Lizzie, cradled there as the wagon rocked and
creaked down the road, gazed at the blue, unchanging sky from
the depths of a new sanctuary: the sweet hole of martyrdom.
The stepmother stroked her brow and the children were all
quiet, respectful of Lizzie's suffering. Lizzie felt a strange, new
sort of happiness—but how hard it would be to win this, over
and over again! And yet, all her life she'd keep trying, in this
very fashion.

Mother schooled her way out of the household, won scholarships to college, earned enough as a teacher to support herself,
all of which built her confidence and later enabled her to guide

our family on where we were to be educated and what we were to aim for in our lives. She had the wherewithal to accomplish her ideas, for during the Depression, hard cash from Father's insurance policies—coupled with our debt-free farm—meant ease in the face of mounting disaster everywhere. We could pull our own way and not swing with the tide of the times. From her experience in the wider world, she knew we ought never lose sight of the fact that one day all of us must leave this community —*and take her too,* though *that* was never said outloud.

Lizzie and Jack, on the contrary, mingled quite freely in local life, attended the neighbors' wedding dances, had fun on bingo nights at the American Legion Club, potluck suppers in the midst of good companionship. On Wednesday bank night at the movies, she and Jack would drive to the Grand Theater to-gether—Mother never along. With Jack's usual luck he won the cash pot often enough to make their moviegoing almost a money-making proposition. Whatever lonely anguish or jealousy Mother suffered, she kept it from showing. Lizzie relished these moments of acting out before the community her man-and-wife pairdom, since so much of our family social life involved rem-nants of relatives—couples weren't emphasized. Mother sus-tained her emotional control by cheerfully postponing daily re-wards and pleasures. What was a movie or a dance compared to the future achievements of each of us, which would give her such ultimate pleasure? *Then* she would live. We were subtly drawn away from interest in local society, except for church doings and the activities of relatives, and were easily attracted to the fine, superior high school in the county seat town, since every-thing of better quality was associated with that community: med-ical service (I'd been born in a hospital there), clothing stores, repair shops. However, because I faced years of orthodontics to correct my undershot jaw, the dentist had to be local. (Soon after my bite was finally perfect and the braces cast aside, the dentist, who'd conscientiously held off until he'd finished the job on my teeth, absconded with another man's wife, leaving his own and four children behind.)

Mother insisted upon setting her college-bred tone to our

training, but while Lizzie lacked book learning, she prided herself in having an uncluttered head when it came to the sure essentials of life. In any tale, she could get to the raw bone fast. She'd fight tenaciously on the bare, stony ground of human needs, whereas Mother took the intellectual's comfort in winning some of her battles in her head or not entering the contest at all. Lizzie's grasp on the present was searingly real, while Mother's imagination projected us into a feeling of what *could* be real for us—tomorrow.

She drew heavily on the remaining insurance money to finance college for her first-born, reasoning that, if he were properly educated and landed a good job, he could help pay for the schooling of us younger ones. Although she was strong in what she wanted for us, she ignored her own needs and only by-the-way mentioned with embarrassment, "I've spent all there was, educating you kids—there won't be anything left, soon. I'm counting on you to support me in my old age," then smiling, blushing, knowing such a statement really needn't be made. Our trust was not to break the faith of the family. When that oldest brother achieved a high-paying professional job, he would remember his responsibilities to the rest of us. All of us knew that. Perhaps without realizing it we were living the American dream. We were such law-abiding, God-fearing, proper-living people we somehow got the idea virtue deserved to be rewarded. *That* was the trouble.

When Mother's health faltered in her fifty-first year (I was thirteen), nothing could stop our tremendous drive forward, for by now the oldest were achieving brilliant records in college—the pattern of deliverance was set. Our family physician, also an accomplished surgeon, operated on her for cancer of the colon and told us he believed he'd "gotten it all," but under the knife she suffered a slight stroke, impairing her speech, partially paralyzing her right side. Now clearly, the primary struggle of her life was over, and what she'd been able to do for us had been done. The rest would be up to each of us. With the excuse of paralysis, the passive side of her personality, held in abeyance by her vigorous determination that the lives of her children would be saved, totally enveloped her. She became like *our* child and was condescended to, in her weakness. But we were flying outward, seldom home. We did not see her invalidism as a burden, and whatever responsibility for her we cherished could remain unplumbed, exertion on her behalf postponed, for Lizzie remained to care for her sister, there in the familiar sanctuary of the old farmstead.

But the nursemaid is also master. Now Lizzie wielded the upper hand and became the single mother of the household, though she adhered to the general guidelines set years before by her sister. Mother lay in a chair by the dining-room radiator, a cat curled at her feet. Day after day she read books from the lending library service of Iowa State College or simply gazed at nothing, her thoughts elsewhere, and gradually drifted into a dark, terrifying corner she could not resist. What if her mind should go? What if it were slipping already? She imagined people were saying unkind things about her at Ladies' Aid and that the minister had her in mind when he spoke of the wicked and lewd. Lizzie regarded these peculiar, paranoid feelings as troublesome, naughty diversions, which Carrie had *better* control. She scolded her sister as one would a small child who'd been bad.

When Cousin Don was killed in an air crash over the Air Force training field in Phoenix, Arizona, Lizzie became the first Gold Star mother in the community. She bore it with trembling, determined lip, in her characteristic way. She refused to crumble under the blow. She'd still prove to God on High that she never deserved this terrible treatment, and He would show compassion yet. For a time, what had been a custom of winter dining-table readings aloud became a nightly devotional hour, with passages from the Bible and church pamphlets. It embarrassed most of us and was dropped after a while, prayer being something too private even for a family. Firmly on the route of serving children, Lizzie couldn't stop because two of her three had died: she kept up the routine for all of us, after the war was over. We mailed laundry bags home from college each week, and she'd send them back loaded with cookies and cake in tinfoil, summer sausages among the socks and handkerchiefs. She nursed Sister Carrie as she'd taken care of her crippled stepmother, the task-to-be like a harness, the fit of which she knew well.

So long as Mother could anticipate the unfurling of events in the lives of us children, her spirit was sustained; she was held together merely by being a witness of destiny. But once the true patterns became evident, and the playing out of our years meant we'd actually be more and more removed from her, a weariness and hopelessness about her own remaining years descended. What was there left to envisage, in her future? Somehow, she'd imagined getting away, too, just as we were doing, but she wouldn't want to be an encumbrance, hang onto us, or interfere in our lives. We were to go off by ourselves without so much as a glance back; otherwise how could we create our lives to their fullest extent? She knew at last the clean, scraped-womb condition of her sacrifice to give us our chance.

As Mother's depression darkened, Lizzie scrutinized her secretly through the glass cupboard doors from the kitchen, noting the weird play of irrationality on the unguarded features, the baleful eyes seeing nothing, the slightly moving lips of a dialogue never to be heard. She was certain worse lay ahead. All Lizzie's life she'd been caring for others, with nothing ever coming to *her,* not even a house of her own, nor clear-title land. What had such benefaction earned her? Two of her three children dead. *Even that which thou hast shall be taken away.* She couldn't help feeling resentful of Carrie's invalidism and particularly angry about the "nonsense" she sometimes spoke. "You keep going like this and you'll end up in Cherokee," she said, threatening the state insane asylum to shock her sister out of her mental difficulties. Now, too, Lizzie began to resist the grooved tracks flung ahead of her: why should *she* be left to nurse her sister, when Carrie had four children old enough to be responsible, even if the oldest of these, who cared the most, seemed the least likely to cope? Our family had always scoffed at misguided people who placed too much emphasis on making money, but now Lizzie realized that, if property settlements had been made long ago and each had gotten his fair share, by this time she and Jack could have accumulated enough to retire to town, as the neighbors' their age were doing. Surely they should have something to show for all these hard years of work! She felt like a sucker.

My sister Ruth and I were the first to marry—the same summer, both weddings in New York with no family in attendance. Mother had met her son-in-law-to-be, but I couldn't afford to bring my fiancée home. There was wartime haste in my marriage plans, for with the Korean conflict widening I was in continual doubt about my Navy reserve status. Mother was unprepared for the final realization of the end of her family closeness to us and said to my next older brother: "Lizzie has Jack, Ruth has her husband, and Curt his wife, but I have no one." She suffered a few fluttering strokes which she kept secret from everyone, and, when she no longer felt capable of holding her mind together, chose to down sleeping tablets rather than be "put away." But, characteristic of suicides, she made known what she'd done quite quickly and was rushed to the Sioux City hospital, where after recovering from the attempt, she was given a series of shock treatments. But the darkness would not leave, and next she tried slashing her wrists—was saved by Lizzie again, and now it was clear she couldn't live at home for some time. Several months later she died of a cerebral hemorrhage from high blood pressure, in the psychiatric ward of the hospital.

Finally, after more than thirty years, Lizzie and Jack became sole masters of the farm, could tailor plans to suit their fancies. Modernization of the kitchen got underway immediately: a new sink, space heater, deep freeze, and an up-to-date light fixture in the fiber-tiled ceiling; china doorknobs were replaced with brushed-brass ones and the wooden kitchen cabinet got a coat of blue paint. Their daughter lived near enough to make frequent trips home, and she was doing so well in her art teacher's career that the years of struggle seemed vindicated. So what if there *was* only one left—she was a gem!

On a routine physical examination, the family physician discovered a spot on Lizzie's lung, said if it were a member of his own family he'd suggest surgery. We all remembered the slight cough she'd always had, particularly in the mornings, and wondered if it were tuberculosis. At the Mayo Clinic, where the operation took place, it was discovered to be a benign tumor; but from the shock of the knife she suffered a stroke, just as her sister had. Part of her mind seemed loose—she couldn't remember the name of her own daughter and yet was aware of the ridiculousness of that. "I *know* you," she'd say, "it's just that I can't think of your name." And later, "What's this piece of meat doing in bed with me? It should be put in the refrigerator—it'll spoil," she said, lifting out her own paralyzed arm.

She lingered in this state for several years, Uncle Jack caretaker and nurse, and daughter Lois hurrying back and forth weekends from her job in order to clean house, wash, cook, help her father in whatever way she could. It was dangerous for her—the old trap of the dutiful daughter—but after her mother's death she moved firmly into her own life and married. Jack lived alone in the farmhouse which had witnessed two generations of teeming life, now as silent as the big, sheltering grove. He could take the sudden emptying because his head was full of all the machines he planned to invent; he was in the good company of his mechanical schemes. There was interesting junk to be found in the yards of the various foundries, a new lathe to buy, and blueprint matters to talk over with his patent lawyer. Someday he might even make a lot of money on an invention, become as successful as all of us now were—in San Francisco, New York, and Los Angeles.

12. Away

The marriage of two brothers and two sisters, who shared their lives and children, created a penumbra of uniqueness which made each child feel his revealed destiny would demonstrate difference. I became the acknowledged future chronicler and composed tales in hot upstairs rooms during the long summers, fed gossip by everyone, for storytelling seemed as plausible a goal as my siblings' claims to concert pianist, airplane pilot, agronomist, and artist. Heavy with the burden of immortality I thought I carried for them, I tried to grasp the reality of our farm world in order to salvage it and leave. Something of this life should live, for in this way one could surmount the pain of promises glimpsed but not realized. Now we have all gone away.

"You seem less like a farmer than anybody I've ever met," people would remark to me. I don't know how much I was trained to achieve this dubious compliment, ranking in my mind with "you don't seem American," which I'd occasionally hear in Iran or England in later years. In truth, I was a dumb farmer, rube, hick, hayseed. The illiterate junk dealer, the lowliest tradesman in town felt superior. His children mocked us because they lived under street lights and had a box at the post office, not R.F.D. Farmers seemed ludicrous to them, smelly and awkward, more familiar with animals than people, couldn't talk. And instead of countering with a pride of occupation, many farmers accepted the attitude, changed to "town clothes" when they had an errand at the bank or grocery store, removed work shoes and stepped into shiny oxfords, took off overalls and drew on trousers with a belt, put on a clean shirt and slicked down unruly hair with water. Towns imposed refinement on crude earth-life. God expected a man to wear his suit to church even in summer, though the fabric was heavy wool.

At high school during noon hour, the farm scholars huddled in their cars to eat cold lunches out of tin boxes, while town classmates trudged home to hot meals and conversation with adults. These city children knew how to cut deep with the sharp edge of discrimination. Their parents—store salesmen, bankers, lawyers, filling-station operators—all lived off the economic creation of the farmer and were subtly contemptuous of him for allowing *them* to reap the middleman's profit. They used brains not muscle, were removed from the degrading physical sweat of body labor. They felt smart.

My father, had he lived, might have joyously accepted rural life and passed it on to us, since he was the first-born son who'd willingly taken over Grandfather's land. But Uncle Jack regarded his lot as a sign of failure: he lingered here on the farm, when with a little education he might have become an engineer. Later, when he acquired two United States patents, one for a snowplow and the other for a device on a corn picker which enabled a man to release jammed ears from the rollers without reaching a hand down—endangering it—he had final proof of what his life's profession might have been.

Sometimes we wondered, What will happen to the farm? Perhaps Cousin Lloyd, who died at eleven, might have carried it on; certainly his brother Don was never interested. Neither were any of Father's sons—except for my oldest brother, who, like Luther Burbank, was a specialist in plant breeding. He could graft an apple tree to produce five different varieties. Although absorbed by the growth processes of flowers and fruit trees, he wouldn't merely settle for the trade aspects of farming.

Science was his love. As a horticulturist, he'd pass far beyond his father's humble achievements. The Agricultural College at Ames was an ideal institution for the sons of this farm generation, long before anyone suspected that corporate agriculture was the future program for Middle West farmlands. The same process that produced trim Fords for not too outrageous a price—the mass creations of the assembly line—would eventually apply to farming as well: bigger and more expensive machinery working larger and larger tracts, and cattle feed lots containing a quarter million dollars "on the hoof" in borrowed money from the bank. The intellectual advance of the "ag" scholar over his farmboy background epitomized progress in the U.S.A.

Our ambitions to leave the land were nurtured by the triumvirate parents, who made our struggle theirs. With German relentlessness we rose each weekday to drive the eleven miles to school, and never, from 1935 until 1945, when we were in attendance, were any of us late, since the kitchen alarm clock was kept an hour or so "fast" and only Lizzie knew *how* fast. We'd sometimes arrive when it was still dark outside the school door, everything locked up, the janitors just beginning to stoke the huge coal furnaces. We were always early because, if a flat tire or other car trouble caused a delay, we'd still be able to make it—perhaps rescued by Jack in another vehicle and carried to the brick school building in time for the first period. Many of us played in the marching band, rehearsals starting at seven forty-five. In winter we were always up by six and starting preparations for the journey, Lizzie fixing our lunchpails and breakfast, Jack coddling the Model A until it exploded into action. The automobile would be warmed up and waiting at the gate, fuming clouds of exhaust in the bitter, below-zero weather. All other farm matters dwindled in importance compared to our educational enterprise. Football practice after school was more important than getting home in time to milk the cows.

Each year in April the high school held a Tuition Party to honor the farm parents who'd made such an effort to lift up their children. We were called "tuition kids" because scholars could attend any school in the county they wished, money from their tax district paid as tuition to the host school. In the Depression this flow helped maintain good science labs and courses such as Latin and German in the college preparatory curriculum, which weren't available in the public high school two miles away, where Father, Uncle Jack, and their sisters had gone.

On Tuition Party night the block-long school was ablaze with lights and filled with hundreds of farmers in their best church clothes. Projects of rural students were on display in the science laboratories, paintings were tacked to the art class walls, the Home Ec girls prepared a supper, and several of us acted in the Tuition Party play. No event of the year was more significant to our family, not even Class Night before Commencement, when senior awards were passed out. (After one such night, Brother Ken, who'd been inducted into the National Honor Society, presented Lizzie with a gold pin in the shape of a palm leaf for having been so relentless in getting us out of bed each morning—and she proudly wore the badge for years.) Our parents met the fabled teachers we talked endlessly about: Mr. Steinjes, the crippled science teacher, whose bright smile and infectious enthusiasm had such an effect upon us; Miss Brink, the black-haired, beautifully speaking English teacher, who loved Shakespeare, coached oral declamation, and directed the major plays; and Mr. Kluckhohn, superintendent, whose cousin, Ruth Suckow, was a famous writer in Mencken's *Smart Set,* and whose other cousin, Clyde, was a leading anthropologist at Harvard. They spoke privately to our parents about us, each sentence plums of reward. A flash of joyous enlightenment passed among us, sustenance for a whole year of academic drudgery. In the great democracy of the intellect, clodhopper backgrounds made no difference; with brains and perseverance any height was attainable.

Aunt Elizabeth suggested and paid for my sister's two years at Stephens College, Columbia, Missouri, the toniest finishing school in the Middle West, where girls not only became cultured and learned the arts of grooming but could take a course in

airplane flying if they wished. Even Peter Pan was flying—
Maude Adams taught in the drama department. My sister must
have felt the farm stigma most cruelly in high school, for by
returning to the remote country each night, what boy could
ask her to the movies, to a school dance? How could he even
find our farm to pick her up or take her home? But at Stephens
she suddenly, miraculously evolved into a beautiful creature.
An arty photographer in Columbia caught the burnished, shining tresses of her perfectly set hair, the star twinkle in her eyes,
and she herself remarked she'd never look prettier. Her voice
became cultivated, her walk poised, and her clothes had that
choice air of debutantism. With calm, new confidence she accepted a job as personal secretary to one of the Hall brothers
at Hallmark greeting cards in Kansas City. After saving enough
to continue toward her degree, she graduated in library science
from the University of Minnesota, married an engineer, and
lives now in California. Her daughter asks me, pulling my un-
calloused city hand, "What was it like on the farm?"

"She's fascinated by the subject," says Ruth, "she can't get
enough of it."

"Tell me—tell me everything."

How can I? It was beautiful to be so much at home, safely
part of an enormous tribe, deep in a country fastness. It was
terrifying to sense the odds against ever climbing out of that
enchanted hole, which we all felt *must* be surmounted. As we
foraged east and west, roaming the nation, "home" was back
there—watching. The farm and surrounding towns remained
physically much the same as decades ago; everything in America
altered quickly, but nothing much changed here, and so we
could always see exactly what we were outdistancing. The farm
served as a gauging point, a harbor for rest—however we needed
to use it in those years when we were beginning to leave. The
welcome from the older generation was mossy, from their repose: "It's here—the same old farm, and all the rest. Glad to
see you but *this* isn't much compared to your exciting life out
there in the world." Our triumphs glowed beyond the rim of
this region, and our elders' pleasure in having us successfully

out of the nest kept us pushed out. They cherished my account of chatting with Dwight D. Eisenhower at the president's reception honoring scholars and fellows at Columbia University, and could scarcely fathom how I managed to attend John Dewey's ninetieth birthday dinner—in the same room with Prime Minister Nehru, Eleanor Roosevelt, Walter Reuther, and other dignitaries.

We all returned to Iowa now and then, especially at the start of our other-life. When I was in the Navy, stationed at Great Lakes and Navy Pier, I'd ride the Hiawatha streamliner home for weekends, twelve hours each way, just to do a little pheasant hunting Sunday mornings and eat home food. And after the shock of Don's death, with the Gold Star flag hanging in our front window, Ken was persuaded to leave the university and take up farming, rather than be drafted and killed too. One son in the family was sacrifice enough for your country. He'd been told by some piano instructor, probably erroneously, that his fingers weren't constructed right for a concert pianist, not a wide enough reach. Uncertain about his music career and shaken by the prospect of war, he farmed for a few months classified 2C by the draft board; but after Iowa City, the life bored him and he felt like a shirker, so he enlisted in the Navy and shipped out to the Pacific. Later, he abandoned music, preferring a sure back-up for making a living, so that he could remain in the big world of other-than-our-Iowa-home. Now a certified public accountant, he and his wife and children live in Southern California.

Cousin Lois, alone of the seven to remain in rural Iowa, did so only after a successful career in the metropolis. Having inherited Jack's ingenuity in making things deftly, she favored the craft side of art, became supervisor of all art instruction in one of Iowa's larger city school systems. With her own apartment, automobile, set of friends, she had everything but a husband. A marriage-broker girl friend who'd happily left spinster-teacher life, found a suitable bachelor living on a farm not far from her, and only forty miles from our old homestead. The first-born of the union, great-great grandson of the pioneer from Germany, was named for the grandfathers, *Jon,* with only a drop of the *h* to indicate modern times. I assumed Uncle Jack would retire and relinquish management of his farm to Lois's husband, for they were tenant farmers in their present location, but she told me firmly no such future was envisioned. She enjoyed the open, progressive atmosphere of her new community and had joined the Methodist church, which was liberal, unoppressive, nothing like the doom-fundamentalism clouding our childhoods. Their neighbors were young farmers-of-the-future, mechanized rural businessmen, and they shared a lively social life. Except for being far from a doctor, such country living had every advantage. Jon and his younger brother Scott attended school only a quarter of a mile away—not walking, however—they insisted upon their modern right to ride the school bus and would hop aboard an hour before classes began, since their farm was the first stop; they'd cruise through the countryside for the sake of disembarking at the schoolhouse steps right along with the other children. Roads were all black-topped and one thought nothing of traveling thirty or forty miles on a shopping errand or to go to a restaurant. Their color television set got most of the same programs and far better reception than my blurry tube in Manhattan. Her rural life was thoroughly transformed from the one experienced as a child; no wonder she wasn't interested in going back home to have memories of late-year sorrows close in, or sense that she alone had not climbed out of the remote country hole where we'd been born.

Sentimentally, I still wondered about our farm's future. Those boys of hers kept gardens, fed pet squirrels, chickens, pigs, and a raccoon, could take apart the hammer mill and put it back together again—these small, lively farmers might someday want the family homestead, wouldn't they? One afternoon when all of us were visiting at "Grandpa Jack's," Jon came crying from behind the house and Lois comforted him, arms open, with a laugh. "What's the matter? Did you get scared again?" And to me: "The big place is too empty—they don't know what to make of it. They get frightened when they find themselves alone, someplace here."

Too many ghosts. But with land so scarce, perhaps in a few years they'll feel differently about the homestead. I said so, aloud, and Lois frowned. "I hope not. I sure don't want them to be farmers. It's too hard a life." And I might have been hearing her mother or my mother saying these very words. Nowadays a farmer couldn't make a living with only two hundred and forty acres. He'd also have to be a large cattle and hog feeder or have a sideline such as trucking. No other laborer in America worked so hard for so little. Her husband grayed early, was developing arthritis, and suffered from an ulcer, probably due to worry over how he was going to manage on the slim margin the market afforded. Little wonder Lois envisioned a different future for her sons; but they have yet to be heard from, with their choices.

I felt I'd been born with a large portion of luck hovering close and generally enjoyed the challenge of the drive-for-success, always secretly believing I'd "win." And yet I never made the highest marks, wasn't well co-ordinated or good at athletics, and sometimes suffered acutely from shyness. But the gilt-edged promise of my tomorrow glowed within me, sustaining me through the bleakest moments. The wife of the music teacher in junior high, dressed up like a gypsy fortuneteller for a school fair benefiting the Band Uniform Fund, gasped when she inspected my strange, simian hand, head and heart line together in a groove like a hinge across the palm. She pronounced me destined for glory. I have since learned that such handprints are found in most birth-defect babies and figure that I was a near-miss idiot for my thirty-eight-year-old mother. Perhaps *that* was the nut of luck I sensed.

Each year I advanced closer to liberation and victory over the binding circumstances of my birth. Too fat, and later in puberty than classmates (or younger, since I began first grade when I was five), I churned for a while in the hell of adolescent anonymity—when the vigor of individuality is buried within the baby fat of "stages," and the sign of a whisker is of utmost importance because your schoolmate already has several. I flayed myself with religious doubts, but since I needed a good relationship with God for "The Power to Win" (the title of a book Aunt Elizabeth gave me for Christmas), I prayed regularly each night before sleep. I performed better as an actor in junior high dramas than on the neophyte basketball team, but played a boy's role well enough to slip under the wire of scrutiny, passed off as regular, and was thereby allowed to nurture a unique self somewhere inside me. I was not burdened with overly watchful home folks, for in a large family there's always privacy somewhere. So long as my activities received community praise, to the adults that's what chiefly counted. Our good deportment was never a question. They knew we didn't lie, steal, or cheat, that Grandfather's moral fervor threaded our chromosomes and nothing regarding "character" had to be spoken of. When fifteen or sixteen and old enough to take out girls, we could drive home at any hour with no questions asked next day, only a little teasing about the lipstick marks on our handkerchiefs, which Lizzie had a hard time scrubbing out in the Monday wash. With the minister peering sternly over one shoulder and Grandpa looming over the other, we were rendered impotent to do anything "bad"—and no wonder we longed to get away.

In high school I learned the upward-mobile routes very quickly and by my senior year was a bona fide member of the leading bunch, a list of activities thick behind my name in the yearbook. To take the College Boards, necessary to win a scholarship to Grinnell (a choice of my own, after talking to the school's representative), I traveled two hundred miles by bus and train, first time on either carrier, and scorned the suggestion from Mother that she accompany me. I was sixteen, surely old enough to be on my own. My state-university-minded family was surprised by this interest in Grinnell, never having heard of the college, but they co-operated with my decision. Money to get me there would come from Father's legacy, so in a way it was my own business. Only once on a vacation home did I pause on my strenuous route to the future to ask

Mother, "Why do we all have to be the *best?* Sometimes it's hard on us!"—which greatly upset her. "No, no, I meant only for you to be happy and enjoy what you do."

She was secretly alarmed over the condition of her oldest, the horticulturist, who could not relax or stop his labors, who seemed obsessive in his scientific researches, found it difficult to allow himself time to be with people "socially," and spoke of having to date as if it were a strange duty he couldn't quite fathom. At eight years old, he had borne the brunt of Father's death and felt the tentative nature of our family predicament in ways that never touched me. The first-born was loaded with responsibility for our welfare, when we attended country school. He'd have the jug of milk and pour it out for all of us, though he served as host absent-mindedly, reading the newspaper in which the lunch had been wrapped—concentratedly. We laughed at how deeply he could become absorbed in his reading, how he'd jump when startled out of it. Miss Crakow at the desk noted his solitary behavior and worried when he preferred to remain in the schoolhouse with her, rather than play bully games at recess. He followed through on all his assigned duties with an agonizing faithfulness and care. He learned to drive tractors and handle farm machinery (but never very well), acquired a school license at age thirteen, in order to operate the Ford. From the first grade on, he was flawless in scholarship and earned all A's. Even about religion he tried to be absolutely correct. Told to believe the fundamentalist concepts, which his scientific mind must have questioned early, he doggedly adhered to the Lutheran line; he willed his faith. In the Christmas season, learning hymns and speeches for the Christmas Eve church pageant was an ordeal for us, but never for him. Delayed by a snowstorm, one Christmas Eve we didn't arrive at the church before services began, and as we entered, up in front of the altar the children were already singing what *he* knew he was supposed to be singing too. Right there in the narthex he burst into song and came singing up the aisle, angel-solemn and pure of face—to move the hearts of the congregation like the Christ child Himself.

I had no intimation of his inner pain, these years, nor did he realize that the torments he endured weren't the private life experience of everybody, the thing-not-said. Mother vigorously championed his advance toward adulthood and self-sufficiency, looking ahead to the time when she could relax her burden—with a man in the family to help share her concern for the younger children. He was salutatorian of his high school class, garlanded with scholarships to college. To have one son an early triumph, and the first-born at that, was the desperate comfort she craved; and he knew the emanations of these unspoken expectations. Upon graduation from the university, highest in Horticulture, second highest in the College of Agriculture, he was quick to inform her of a spectacular job offer from Hawaii, an impressive salary and far enough away from Iowa to assure her that paradise was coming within reach. Of course, the pineapple growers would have liked to make commercial use of his learning, but he chose pure science and decided to continue toward a Ph.D. But earlier, during the war, on a steamy island battleground of the South Pacific, where he served in the Medical Corps, he had suffered a breakdown. Under the strain of graduate study the old afflictions had descended. And now, these many years of his hospitalization, as he works daily in the greenhouse on the grounds, he dwells in the time of his promise, those years of the 1930's, remembering the location of each grape arbor and fruit tree on the farm, what kind of soil can be found on every acre. Even this language is faithful to the period. His lost childhood remains a tantalizing dream he cannot relinquish. I write my way out of the same obsessions to have done with them. And to see to it that the dreams we all dreamt then in some measure come true.

Cousin Don was physically endowed with his father's good male body, big in the shoulders, lean in the hips, sexy, and although one leg was an inch shorter than the other, he walked so that nobody could tell and played football like a champion, winning the praise of Jack. The jockstraps swinging from the clothesline on washday signaled to us all the new man in the family. Women knew a handsome winner when they saw one,

and he could date any of the sleek, sophisticated town girls
even though he lived on a farm. He was a spiffy dresser, nothing
of the hayseed about him. He accomplished his assigned chores
on the land—cultivating corn in June, haying, or threshing—
with a shrug and not too much interest. While his city pals
lay around in the sun at the WPA swimming pool, created
out of a sand pit near the county seat town, Don drove the
tractor garbed in brief, satinized bathing trunks, limbs greased
in order to achieve a comparable tan—much to the astonishment
of the hidebound neighbors driving past on the way to town.
The moaning view of life, with clouds of sin, gloom, and a
sense of human unworthiness—and longing for eternal rewards
—which filled the church and somewhat cast a shadow over
our household, did not faze him. His body told him different
news. "Look at the shoulders on him," an admiring parent
would say, or "you're getting to be a real man," all of which he
accepted with indolent self-congratulation.

He was playful and irreverent with us younger children. At
the pool, since we hadn't yet been enrolled for swimming lessons,
we had to stay behind the ropes in safe water. He'd play water
polo with us, teasing us by hiding the ball—one time so successfully we couldn't find it anywhere. Then I spotted it stuffed
in his groin and lunged. He let out a yowl that alarmed the
lifeguards high on their white wooden platforms. "Don't you
ever grab me there again!" he warned, a sick look on his face.
Although his voice was deep and he shaved twice a week, I
hadn't been aware of his sexual change and didn't understand
it. Not long afterward we were in the two-hole outhouse together
and he showed me for enlightenment what he looked like now,
quickly rising to erection. Amazed, when I returned to the
mulberry trees where the family was picking up shaken-down
mulberries from old bed sheets on the ground, I announced
that he had "a big red sausage" until he slapped me down.
With high school girls terrified of becoming pregnant and worried lest they get the reputation of being "too fast," which
would hinder them from landing a suitable husband, few boys
got far under their skirts. But at college Don found lovely,

susceptible girls and on vacations he'd allude to his conquests, me the recipient of these accounts because of our long-ago outhouse intimacy. He helped free me from puritanical inhibitions about sex; I idolized his dashing ways and now yearned for not only occupational renown but serious achievements in lovemaking as well.

As I attained high school age, I lost fat and could fit into most of Cousin Don's castoff college wardrobe. He chose me as if I were his younger brother and heir apparent, instructing me in grooming, how to tie a Windsor knot, how to co-ordinate trousers and sports coat, select the proper shirt. He and my sister taught me to dance. I inherited his gray herringbone suit, which I was to wear with his bittersweet woven wool cravat—a tie I still have in my closet and occasionally wear. He sensed in me early signs of a streak of luck, for I was good enough looking to date the prettiest girls, could look sharp and yet remain properly calm. We didn't have to discuss these affinities or try to define them; it might tempt misfortune if we did. But in the cards all the aces seemed about to turn up for us— glamour, riches, girl friends—and our bond was the secret of sexuality, openly accepted, whereas others in the family kept it remote and unexamined.

Don may have enlisted in the Army Air Corps soon after the attack on Pearl Harbor because he'd look so well in the trim lines of the beige-pink officer's trousers and dark brown coat, but he'd also been mad about airplanes from an early age. He once built a gasoline-engine model four and a half feet long, which achieved only one flight before it crashed into the barnyard. Odors of banana glue filled the attic, where he worked putting balsa parts together. And from airplane magazines he snipped out every model illustrated he could find, scotch-taping them to the wall over his bedstead, an entire wallpapered corner all in colors, bright planes in blue skies—while across the room my oldest brother had over *his* head a copy of Gainsborough's *Blue Boy*.

When Don was killed in a mid-air collision over Phoenix, Arizona, while still in training, the blow shattered us each in different ways. Because the coffin remained closed during the funeral, I hoped there'd been a dreadful mistake and we'd hear news of him before long. Or, perhaps the honor guard sent by the Air Corps, such a handsome, kindly lieutenant, would remain connected to our family, fall in love with Ruth, and marry her. My next-older brother often told me that the death by appendicitis of Cousin Lloyd eased the German severity of our upbringing—no more whippings with the razor strop in the washroom. But this newest obliteration profoundly dented the rosy certainty of our drive toward the future. "Damn that Hitler!" Mother cried, her first words after the telegram arrived by mail carrier, and we all stood there in the kitchen, stunned— that March afternoon in 1943. She now perceived how the current of the times would play havoc with the scheme of the future set for us—all the effort might come to nothing. But didn't we deserve to have everything turn out right for us? In the face of adversity she and the family had behaved gallantly, putting energies and resources in the right place. Most people burned up their chances along with their lives, getting what they could from the moment, but we had built patiently, constructively. What sense could be made of such horrible dealings by fate—how were we to regard God? The sorrow of Jack and Lizzie was too deep for lamentation and too private scarcely to be shown. Like all persons honored by tragedy, an unreal, sleepwalking glow seemed to entomb them wherever they went. They were regarded with awe, for what they were enduring.

As soon as possible I tried to sound a last chord to make the balance, to proclaim the untruth that life isn't tragedy—and that we'd prevailed and "won." When Mother was confined to the psychiatric ward of a hospital, afflicted also with high blood pressure which might trigger a final stroke (the doctor saying she "could go at any time"), I made a trip home after having been away a full year and a half (married now and set up in a New York apartment), to present myself and my life to her, for her reward, before that "final reward" so much in doubt. I'd been working for the United Nations Secretariat but had recently resigned in order to accept a contract in college teaching. She was eager to lay eyes upon my wife, not to approve or disapprove, since my judgment in these matters would stand, but merely to witness what was happening to me. In our meeting she recognized the full drama of the moment. Her eyes teared happily as she clutched my hand in hers and reached for my wife's hand. The one thing she wanted me to understand surely was that now my life had completely fulfilled the sacrifices of hers—I should be nourished and draw strength from her corpse of a life, just as corn plants grow strong when rooted in the carcass of a pheasant. She enumerated the facts making up this achievement: I was now actually a university teacher, about to earn the magnificent salary of $3600 a year, had a home of my own, and I'd married the prettiest girl imaginable. After her picture appeared in the society column of the town newspaper with a write-up making us seem so interesting and glamorous, many friends and relatives had told Mother I "sure knew how to pick 'em." Finally meeting my wife, she saw what she wanted to see and flushed with joy. We made the sincere offer of suggesting she live with us for a while if she ever got well enough to leave the hospital. When she died a few months later I experienced the only profoundly psychic moment of my life. I leapt out of the bed in the middle of the night as if thrown by a terrific force. My wife asked, "What's the matter? Where are you going?" I found myself standing in the hall and said automatically, "Someone's calling." Next morning my brother phoned to say Mother had died at the very hour in the night I'd been propelled from bed. Yes, I was close to my mother, but only at the moment of death did she pull me by that choking umbilical cord—the rest of the time I was allowed to run free as if born to be my own man, no one having a claim upon me except myself. For that second gift of life from my mother, I've been grateful.

She divested herself of her four offspring in order to save us; *that* was why we were all to go away. Almost mystically, she had a sense of launching us into the mainstream of future American life, for we would die if we remained where we were born. She'd seen too many people stunted and shriveled by their lack of a chance to make of themselves all that might have been coming to them. She seized upon education as the magic weapon, and although she never said such a fatuous thing, certainly believed any of us could be President if we wished. Oddly enough, she was right. As our minds and bodies grew, we were companions for her loneliness, able to talk with her about world politics, Tolstoi, and Willa Cather, for there were no other people with whom to discuss intellectual matters; she had no college-educated friends of her own. She understood that we must seek out like-minded individuals, who were to be found in larger towns and cities, for our intellectual growth.

The land here might nourish our bodies, build stamina and spirit, but in our progress through the years, it too would have to be left behind for what it could never do for us. The mindlessness of Nature would erode our ambitions to hurl ourselves into life and make our marks. Only in a man-made environment —the city—could one forget the humdrum futility of the years in passage. The illusion that there was a lot to *do* in life besides merely *being* in life could only be sustained in an urban setting. In this way our generation, using the mulched dead matter of agrarian life like projectile fuel for our thrust into the future, became part of that enormous vitality springing out of rural America.